D0267616

CURIOSITIES
OF
POLITICS

JONATHAN RICE

CARTOONS BY ROBERT DUNCAN

FOR MY WIFE, JAN, A VOTE OF CONFIDENCE

First published in Great Britain in 1995 by
PAVILION BOOKS LIMITED
26 Upper Ground, London SE1 9PD

Designed by Nigel Partridge

A CIP catalogue record for this book is available from the British Library

ISBN 1 85793 350 8

Typeset in Sabon
Printed and bound in the U.K. by Hartnolls Ltd

2 4 6 8 10 9 7 5 3 1

CONTENTS

INTRODUCTION

After *Curiosities of Cricket* and *Curiosities of Golf*, why Politics? There's no quick answer to that, although the thought first came into my mind when I considered the career of Ted Dexter, who as a cricketer was Captain of England and later Chairman of Selectors, as a golfer has won the President's Putter on two occasions, but as a politician was less of a winner. He stood against James Callaghan as the Conservative candidate in the 1964 general election, but failed to trouble the scorers to any great extent. Clearly, despite Robert Louis Stevenson's assertion that 'politics is the only profession for which no preparation is thought necessary', the successful practice of politics is rather difficult.

One of the remarkable features of cricket and golf, and most other sports, is that true devotees of these pastimes are more than just interested in them; they are fanatical about them. The same can be said of politics. It's not government, or the small print of Acts of Parliament which fascinate, it is the people who make themselves look anything from splendid to daft in their pursuit of political influence. That's what keeps mere spectators at the game of politics so interested in the way it is being played. All over the world, people are passionately interested in politics, a fact underlined by a news report from New Zealand in 1964: 'After crashing their car, Mr Shepherd and Mr Donaldson, who are on holiday from the United States, were surrounded by passers-by. Streaming with blood and badly bruised, they faced a barrage of questions like "Who did you vote for in the last election?" and "Will Governor Romney become President?"'

Such passion breeds eccentricity. Politics, being something that shapes our lives but which apparently requires no special skills to understand, is an activity which attracts glorious eccentrics as north attracts south. Curiosities abound. As Disraeli commented many years ago, 'What we anticipate seldom occurs; what we least expect generally happens.'

My opinion of politics as a source of curiosities was confirmed by an Irish political commentator who said, in the uncertain weeks at the end of 1994 when Albert Reynolds was finally forced to resign as Prime Minister, 'We treat politics as the greatest spectator sport yet invented, so everybody is enjoying the crisis immensely.' It is always worth remembering that even though politics is so often a matter of life and death for the participants, it isn't really a matter of life and death.

Politics is, however, a vast subject, so obviously some limits had to be imposed on the hunt for curiosities. Firstly, I decided to deal only in what can broadly be termed modern politics, from around 1860 onwards. This encompasses British politics from the Gladstone/Disraeli era and the development of modern party politics; it includes American political life since the Civil War; Japan and East Asia only after the arrival of the Western powers, and Continental Europe from the age of Bismarck onwards. It was also decided to deal only with politics at a national level. Local politics, which in most countries is one vast curiosity, is not covered, except where local affairs have developed into national curiosities. Finally, I have tried to keep a distinction between politics and war, and between politics and diplomacy. Thus I have not tried to look at political decisions in wartime, for example, nor at the activities of the diplomatic services of the world. The tragic story of Edwin Reischauer, US Ambassador to Japan, who in 1964 was stabbed at the American Embassy by a Japanese fanatic, will not be found in the chapters which follow. (He was rushed to Toranomon Hospital near the embassy and made a good recovery from the stabbing. However, he caught hepatitis from an infected blood transfusion.) Nor will you read of the King of Hawaii who in March 1881 visited Japan seeking a member of the Imperial Japanese family as a consort for his daughter. (He returned empty-handed.) Royalty and diplomats have their own extraordinary penchant for acting curiously, but that is another book or two.

I hope also that my own political opinions, such as they are, will not be apparent from the way the book is put together. I have made no attempt to check whether there are more stories from the right than from the left of the political spectrum, or vice versa. To me it does not matter. I have no political points to make, although I will go on record as saying that I would rather live under a government led by Margaret Thatcher or Harold Wilson or Ronald Reagan or Bill Clinton than one led by the heirs to Leonid Brezhnev, Kim Il Sung or Enver Hoxha. And they all know how to make me laugh.

JONATHAN RICE, February 1995

A COCKTAIL OF PARTIES

The two driving forces of mankind are, it is said, the desire for territory and the sexual urge, the possession of which defines our concept of power. So it is perhaps not surprising that politics, the art of wielding power without usually inflicting physical damage, is one in which territory and sex play a significant part. Territory differs from sex in that it is not always physical, although the basic territorial and political entity, the nation state, is defined as much by its geographical area as by its economic or spiritual shape. Territory is mental as well, just as sex is if you're on your own. Territory is an ideal, a set of principles by which any human, but most frequently a politician, will claim to live.

Defending a physical territory may well be a male preserve (and the root cause of most wars through the ages), but defending a set of principles is something that both sexes try to do. In the male sex this taking of the spiritual high ground is known as being pompous, and with the female sex it is known as nagging. However, defending a territory successfully, or attacking somebody else's territory with any real hope of victory, is something that is usually beyond the powers of one man on his own, whether we are talking of abstract or concrete territorial waters. So it has tended to be a team event, rather than an individual one, ever since the game was invented, which was almost as soon as man developed any powers of communication. Politics has a strong claim to being the oldest profession of all, although in the early days politicians were probably enthusiastic amateurs rather than paid entertainers. But whether it was originally a spin-off from amateur dramatics or a highly lucrative business, politics was always the domain of teams of strolling players rather than the individual stand-up comic. Even the ancient Chinese played politics as a party game, and in the past century and a half the rules have been defined and refined by the Western democracies, as though they were setting out the rules of golf or rugby football.

Nowadays, we tend to think of American politics as revolving around two parties, the Republicans and the Democrats, while in Britain there are two and a half, the Conservatives, the Labour Party and the Liberal Democrats. In most European democracies there are two or three main political groupings – of left, centre and right – while for 75 years in most of Eastern Europe there was only one political party, the Communist Party. Even today, there are many countries which are one-party states: quite probably a majority of the almost 200 separate countries that have achieved membership of the United Nations are governed by a parliament in which there is no loyal opposition, which shows that politicians all over the world love to get together and tell each other how wonderful they are. Except when they are telling their political opponents how unspeakable they are.

Joining a political party is the first step towards becoming a politician. It is pretty well impossible to be elected to the parliament of any free democracy without announcing one's allegiance to one of the major political parties. Of course, it is not necessary to stay joined to the same party for your entire political life, as many successful politicians from Winston Churchill (both Liberal and Conservative in a 60-year career as a Member of Parliament) to John Horam have found out. Horam, Conservative MP for Orpington in Kent from 1992, was previously Labour MP for Gateshead West before defecting to the Social Democratic Party in 1981 and representing until 1983 the good citizens who had elected him as a solid Labour member two years earlier. Reg Prentice was elected as Labour member for East Ham North in May 1957 and rose to the rank of Secretary of State for Education and Science in the Labour administration 17 years later. In October 1977 he changed sides, and two years later was sitting on the Government front benches again, this time as Conservative MP for Daventry and Minister for Social Security. By 1987 he was the Rt Hon. Sir Reginald Prentice.

In America, Charles Sumner, who was elected to the Senate as a Democrat in 1851 but later switched to the Republicans, was neither the first nor the last to change sides. Governor John Connally of Texas, the man who was injured by Lee Harvey Oswald when Kennedy was assassinated, was at that time a Democrat. By the time he died 30 years later, he was a leading member of the Republican Party. Senator Strom Thurmond was elected Governor of South Carolina in 1946 as a Democrat. He stood as presidential candidate for the States Rights Party in 1948 against Truman and Dewey, winning four southern states. In 1954 he was elected to the Senate as a Democrat without his name appearing on the ballot paper. He joined the Republican Party in 1964 and in 1994 became Chairman of the Senate Armed Services Committee at the age of 92.

There have been politicians who have reached the highest peaks without professing any real allegiance to any party. Ulysses S. Grant, the Civil War general, was nominated by the Republican Party as their presidential candidate in 1868, despite the fact that he had only ever once voted in a presidential election, and then for the Democratic candidate. Despite this rather poor track record, or maybe because of it, the American public twice elected him as their President. In 1868, it must be admitted, the options were not particularly impressive. Grant's Democratic opponent, Horatio Seymour, who had been Governor of New York, had said repeatedly and in public that he did not have 'the slightest desire to occupy the White House; there is too much trouble and responsibility'. In an attempt to ensure that he could not be nominated, he took on the chairmanship of the Democratic convention. When his name was put forward despite his strong opposition, he told the convention that he must not be nominated 'as I could not accept the nomination if tendered'. Twenty ballots later, when the convention was still deadlocked, his name was reintroduced, still against Seymour's wishes. He repeated forcefully that he meant it when he said he was not a candidate, but then made the fateful error of leaving the convention for a few minutes to get a breath of fresh air. While he was outside the convention hall, the delegates nominated him, and so Horatio Seymour stood for the presidency. No doubt to his immense personal relief, he failed to beat General Grant, who, however, had he maintained a consistent voting record in presidential elections, would presumably have voted for his opponent.

Grant was not the only political neophyte to have been nominated for the presidency. General Dwight D. Eisenhower was courted by both major parties, who needed a war hero to lead them to the White House, despite the fact that neither party had any real idea what Eisenhower's political views were. He chose the Republicans and duly served eight years as President. It is said that Herbert Hoover was sounded out by both parties in 1920, but when he indicated that he would accept a Republican offer, they promptly nominated Warren Harding, safe in the knowledge that Hoover would not run against their man. It was eight years before Hoover became the Republican nominee (and shortly afterwards President).

Some politicians are remarkably cavalier about the way they embrace a particular political creed. President Houphouet-Boigny of the Ivory Coast was known throughout the 33 years of his presidency as a very conservative politician. Yet when he was elected to the French parliament immediately after the Second World War, he sat as a Communist. When the newly elected deputies from the far reaches of the French Union reached Paris, they quickly realized that they would have very little influence unless they were members of a mainland political party and could work within the system. Several French Union members drew lots to see which party they would ally themselves to, and Houphouet-Boigny drew the Communist Party. It is not always possible to tell a political book by its cover.

Nor is it possible to work out who will govern you, even after the election has been held. The good citizens of Mauritius were faced in 1987 with a complicated choice. They could vote again for the Mouvement Socialiste Mauricien and Prime Minister Sir Aneerood Jugnauth, or they could vote for the

Labour Party (MLP), the Social Democratic Party of Mauritius (PMSD) or indeed the Organisation du Peuple Rodriguais (OPR). Then again, they could put their cross against the Mouvement Militant Mauricien candidate. The 70 seats at stake were bound to yield a wide cross-section of opinion and provoke lively parliamentary debate. Or not. The result was that the election was won by a coalition of the MSM, the MLP, the PMSD and the OPR. The only set of letters doomed to opposition was the MMM. The coalition had a comfortable majority of 22 seats, and cordial agreement reigned. Then in August 1988 the PMSD broke ranks and went into opposition, with the MMM. Two years later, in September 1990, the MLP also broke from the governing coalition, which would have left just the MSM and the OPR in power, had not the MMM decided at the same time to change sides, and move *into* the coalition. From being the devils incarnate, the MMM suddenly became a vital part of the governing coalition, whose policies did not seem to change very much. Half of those parties who had held firmly pro-Government views a year or two earlier were now members of the loyal opposition, and Sir Aneerood Jugnauth still held office. Quite what the voters thought of all this was uncertain until Sir Aneerood held another general election in September 1991. He won again. By this time the voters had worked out that it did not really matter which party you chose to vote for. It would still be bound to spend some time in power and some time in opposition, unless it was led by Sir Aneerood, in which case it would always be in power.

The Liberal Democratic Party *(Jiyu Minshuto)* of Japan has spent little time in opposition, whoever has been the leader.

It is often likened to the Holy Roman Empire, which has been described as being neither Holy nor Roman nor an Empire – but otherwise aptly named. The Liberal Democratic Party of Japan is neither liberal (being a right-wing conservative organization) nor democratic (being a power broker's paradise where smoke-filled rooms take the place of the ballot-box) nor a party (being originally an amalgam of two separate parties and nowadays a loose federation of several mutually distrusting factions), but despite all this, it retained power in Japan for almost 50 years. For many years Japanese politics had two political sides: the Liberal Democratic Party on the right and the Socialists and the Communists on the left. The Clean Government Party *(Komeito)* stood rather wistfully somewhere between these two extremes, but had little opportunity to show whether or not it could live up to its name, as it never had any chance of participating in government, clean or dirty. Suddenly, in 1993, a general election threw the LDP out of office, and a mass of minor parties formed an uneasy coalition government. Japan nowadays has more political parties than any other major democracy, with new parties appearing to spring up every time an LDP politician decides there is more fun in being a big fish in a small pond. Most of the parties represented in the Lower House of the Diet are cuttings taken from the LDP tree, but their most difficult policy decision seems to be how to name the party so that the electorate has some idea of what they stand for. The Japan Renewal Party *(Shinseito)* has provided a Prime Minister recently, Mr Tsutomu Hata, but as Japan has more living ex-Prime Ministers than any other nation, this is not proof that the Japan Renewal Party is stronger than the rest of the pack. The Japan New Party *(Nihon Shinto)* is entirely different. It also has an ex-Prime Minister in its ranks, but includes former members of the LDP and the Social Democratic Federation *(Shaminren)*. The Democratic Socialist Party *(Minshu Shakaito)*, which draws its support from the union-based Friendly Society *(Yuaikai)*, must not be confused with the Social Democratic Party *(Nihon Shakaito)*, which until recently was officially translated as the Japan Socialist Party, but its leaders decided that a name like that might give the wrong impression to those who cannot speak Japanese. There is also a Liberal Party *(Jiyuto)*, which is nothing to do with the Liberal Democratic Party, and which has roughly 200 fewer MPs. There is a group of four MPs who call themselves the Former 'Reform Group' *(Kyu-Kaikaku no Kai)*, which implies that they are no longer interested in reform, but actually they are just interested in being part of the governing coalition while retaining an identity of their own, however curious that identity might be. The New Harbinger Party *(Shino Sakigake)* and the New Future Party *(Shinto Mirai)* are, needless to say, completely different in their political values and policies, even though many less well-educated Japanese voters can scarcely tell the difference. The Japan Communist Party *(Nihon Kyosanto)* carries on blithely despite the collapse of Communism almost everywhere, and boasts 15 MPs, which is 12 more than the strangely but entirely frankly named Ambition Group (*Gurupu Aogumo,* which literally means 'Blue Cloud Group', but they prefer the official translation which shows they want to succeed, even if the entire electorate knows they will not). At the very end of 1994 two new parties appeared on the scene, one with the naïvely charming name of *Shinshinto,* which translates as the New New Party. The official English name of the party is actually the New Frontier Party, but on closer inspection it turns out to be a Tired Old Party after all. It is the creation of a powerful ex-LDP backroom fixer, Ichiro Ozawa and its leader is ex-LDP Prime Minister Toshiki Kaifu. The other new party was altogether less naïvely named, being called the AV Party. AV stands for 'Able Volunteer', according to the official hand-outs, but as AV is also Japlish shorthand for 'Adult Video', and the party's founder is a Japanese porn star called Anri Inoue, we can assume that sexual politics has finally reached Japan. Its main campaign platform is to stop discrimination against the sex industry, citing the fact that women identified as sex industry workers cannot get bank loans or even credit cards in Japan. The AV Party, not being an offshoot of the Liberal Democratic Party, does not yet have any members of the Japanese Diet.

Japanese politics is not getting any easier to understand, and that understanding is not helped by their peculiar system of multi-member constituencies, which forces even candidates

of the same party standing in the same constituency to emphasize their differences rather than their similarities in order to ensure they are elected. Oh for the days of the illiberal, undemocratic Liberal Democratic Party, when the politicians got on with debating issues in parliament and collecting money, and the bureaucrats got on with running the country.

Liberal Democrats seem to invite confusion around the world. At the European elections in June 1994 a 50-year-old retired headmaster, Mr Richard Huggett, stood in the constituency of Devon and East Plymouth as a Literal Democrat, in opposition to Mr Adrian Sanders, a Liberal Democrat. There was also Mr Giles Chichester, the son of round-the-world yachtsman Sir Francis Chichester, who was standing in the Conservative cause. When the votes were all counted and recounted, Mr Chichester had a majority of just 700 votes over the Liberal Democrat. Mr Huggett picked up 10,203 votes, by far the largest vote ever for a candidate unaffiliated to any known party, and the Liberal Democrat quite naturally cried 'Foul'. His argument was based on the fact that the name Huggett comes before Sanders alphabetically and therefore was listed higher on the ballot papers. The Lib Dems were claiming, in effect, that the politically naïve voters of Devon and Plymouth East must have voted for Mr Huggett rather than Mr Sanders because they could not read and/or because the Liberal Democrat candidate had made so little impression on the loyal party voters that they had no idea what his name was anyway. Mr Huggett distributed no election leaflets and took part in only two public meetings during the campaign, but still caused over 10 per cent of the potential Liberal Democrat voters to put their cross against his name, which makes one wonder why the Lib Dems actually wanted the votes of such an ignorant electorate, part of whom had returned Mr Alan Clark as their Member of Parliament for 18 years. The matter was referred to the High Court, where the Liberal Democrats tried to have the election declared void, but their appeal failed. Mr Chichester, who won only 14.3 per cent of the votes of the entire electorate as the turn-out was only 45.1 per cent, remains MEP for Devon and Plymouth East. The lesson for the Liberal Democrats is to choose candidates from the upper one-third of the alphabet: their Mr Sanders (coincidentally the name under which Winnie the Pooh lived in *The House at Pooh Corner*) was the eighth name on a list of eight candidates, while Mr Chichester was the first. Until a Conservative candidate stands damagingly in an election, when the rules will probably be changed, all candidates hoping to be elected in a multi-candidate election should give themselves names like Aardvark or Ashdown or Blair or Clinton. In 1994 there were 27 British MPs with names beginning with the letter A, but only three beginning with the letter Y and none with the letters X or Z.

Liberal Democracy still does not extend to all parts of the world. There are still several states that are not only not governed by a Liberal Democratic Party, they do not even have such a party within their system. They have names which to our sophisticated political ears sound silly. We, who are used to choosing between parties with sensible names like Labour, Conservative, Gremloids and Christian Socialist Opposing Secret Masonic Government, find it hard to take seriously names like the Radical Civil Union, the Congress Party, the United Workers' Party, the People's Party, the Union of Democratic Forces, the Christian Democratic Union, the National Front for Change and Democracy and the Nationalist Republican Alliance, all of whom have held power somewhere during the past few years.

There seems to be no clear-cut way of giving a party the right name to appeal to the voters and be successful at the polls, at least not since the collapse of Communism. It does not even really help to have an exciting name promising forceful leadership and great things in the future. The National Union for the Total Independence of Angola (UNITA) has the sort of name you would think would sum up the aspirations of a former African colony looking for self-respect, but they have consistently failed to win power, perhaps because their Total Independence seems to depend on the support of the United States and South Africa. At the other end of the inspiring name spectrum, just look at the results of the 1988 Swedish general election. It was won, as nearly always, by the Social Democrats (156 seats), followed by the Moderates (66 seats), the Liberals (44 seats), the Centre Party (42 seats), the Communists (21 seats) and the Greens (20 seats). Getting excited over the

campaign and the outcome of that election with that particular selection of runners must have taxed the ingenuity of even the most skilful Swedish political commentator. How can it be possible in Sweden (population 8.8 million) to have not only a Liberal Party, internationally a name implying centrist policies, but also a Moderate Party and a Centre Party? Is there a phrase in Swedish which means, 'I do not agree'? If there is, it can never have been used by any of their politicians. Nor in Barbados, for that matter. In 1991 the outcome of the Bajan general election was that of the 28 seats in the House of Assembly, 18 went to the Democratic Labour Party and the remaining 10 went to the Barbados Labour Party. No other shade of political opinion was represented.

Generally speaking, in all countries and in all languages, the words 'Democratic' and 'Union' seem to be popular, with 'National' close behind. The word 'Revolutionary' has recently gone out of fashion, while 'Green' seems to have been a word for the 1980s. A National Democratic Union party, or a Union for National Democracy, has generally, when given the chance, been in with a shout with most sets of electors, although only a few have actually taken the reins of power. There are slight variations available, of course, such as the United Democratic Party in Belize, the National Democratic Congress in Grenada, the United National Party in Sri Lanka and the Kenyan African National Union, which is the only party in Kenya. Turkey has a Motherland Party, and Afghanistan a Homeland Party. Their names tell us little about their policies, however.

Finally, there are the parties named after a particular politician and embodying his or her ideals and beliefs, but they very rarely outlive their founder. There are exceptions, notably the Perónists (named after President Juan Perón) in Argentina, the Zapatists (after Emiliano Zapata) in Mexico, the Sandinistas (after Augusto César Sandino) in Nicaragua, and even the RPR (Rassemblement pour la République), informally known as the Gaullists (after General de Gaulle) in France. The Zapatists, incidentally, are just one of the parties up against the most oxymoronically named political party in the world, the ruling Institutional Revolutionary Party. How can anything be both institutional and revolutionary? Politics and honesty rarely meet. These days, however, political leaders prefer to be known for their own -isms rather than as synonyms for a political party. Thatcherism, Reaganomics and Butskellism (that odd amalgam of the remarkably similar policies in the 1950s of the reforming Tory Chancellor Rab Butler and his Socialist predecessor Hugh Gaitskell) are part of the political dictionary these days, even though the parties at the centre of power in Britain and the United States are still known by the names they have lived under for generations.

The Whigs and the Tories, names that have been applied

to Britain's two main political parties for at least 300 years, were originally derogatory terms. 'Whig' was a Scottish word for a horse thief and 'Tory' was an Irish term for an outlaw. It was almost inevitable, therefore, that they should be applied to political parties, even before the Whigs decided to call themselves Liberals and the Conservative Party was formed out of an alliance of the land-owning Tories. Tories are still in charge in Britain, and four US Presidents officially described themselves as Whigs, but were probably what we would now describe as Republican. There has never been a Tory President of the United States, even though Ronald Reagan, for one, would have fitted snugly into the Conservative Party if he had been British.

SUPPLEMENTARIES

Parties that have been represented at British elections:

Belgrano Bloodhunger: Benjamin Wedmore, 13 votes at Finchley, 1983

Blancmange Thrower: Ms P. H. Stephenson, 328 votes at Windsor and Maidenhead, 1987

Buy Your Chesterfields in Thame: D. Butler, 24 votes at Chesterfield, 1984

Chauvinist Raving Alliance Party: Christchurch, 1992

Christian Socialist Opposing Secret Masonic Government: A. B. Shone, 125 votes at Reading East, 1987

Common Market No Hanging Yes: W. O. Smedley, 217 votes at Saffron Walden, 1987

Creek Road Fresh Bread Party: G. W. Fuller, 373 votes at Havant, 1987

Elvisly Yours Elvis Presley Party: Sid Shaw, 20 votes at Chesterfield, 1984

End Unemployment Vote Justice For Jobless Party: Sheffield Central, 1992

Eurobean From the Planet Beanus: Captain Beany, 1,106 votes at South Wales West, Euro-elections 1994

European People's Party Judo (sic) Christian Alliance: Giovanni Sabrizi, 880 votes at London North, Euro-elections 1994

Fancy Dress Party: K. J. Davenport, 491 votes at Dartford, 1987; Alan Munro, 262 votes at Dartford, 1992

Four-Wheel Drive Hatchback Road Safety: David Bentley, 116 votes at Chesterfield, 1984

Jolly Small Brewers Party: Worcester, 1992

Let's Have Another Party Party: N. D. Byles, 209 votes at Exeter, 1987

MCCARTHY – Make Criminals Concerned About our Response To Hostility and Yobbishness: George Harrison, 3,693 votes at Greater Manchester West, Euro-elections 1994

National Teenage Party: Lord David Sutch, 208 votes at Stratford-upon-Avon, 1963

No Increase in Dental Charges: J. Davey, 83 votes at Chesterfield, 1984

Official Acne Party: Giancarlo Picarro, 15 votes at Chesterfield, 1984

Official Loony Monster Green Chicken Alliance: Jeremy Stooks, 177 votes at Poole, 1983

Official Monster Raving Loony Party: Lord David Sutch, over thirty times, from 1982

Only Official Best Party Candidate: C. D. Slee, 435 votes at Bedfordshire North, 1987

Private Eye Party: Willie Rushton, 45 votes at Kinross & West Perth, 1963

Public Safety Democratic Monarchist White Resident: Lt. Com. W. Boaks, 5 votes at Glasgow Hillhead, 1982

RABIES – Rainbow Alliance Brixton Insane Extremist Sect: F. M. Jackson, 171 votes at Norwood, 1987

Real Bermondsey Labour: John O'Grady, 2,243 votes at Bermondsey, 1983

Tactical Voting Annihilates Bennite Thatcherites: Thomas Keen, 27 votes at Darlington, 1983

Up the Creek Have a Party: Greenwich, 1992

Women, Life on Earth and Ecology Party: Simone Wilkinson, 279 votes at Finchley, 1983

657 Party: R. Hughes, 455 votes at Portsmouth South, 1987

Elected for more than one party:

Aidan Crawley, Labour MP for Buckingham 1945–51, Conservative MP for West Derbyshire 1962–7

Roy Jenkins, Labour MP for Central Southwark 1948–50, Stechford 1950–76, Social Democrat MP for Glasgow Hillhead 1982–7

Evelyn King, Labour MP for Penryn and Falmouth 1945–50, Conservative MP for South Dorset 1964–79

David Owen, Labour MP for Plymouth Sutton 1966–74, Plymouth Devonport 1974–81, Social Democrat MP for Plymouth Devonport 1981–92

Shirley Williams, Labour MP for Hitchin 1964–74, Hertford and Stevenage 1974–9, Social Democrat MP for Crosby 1981–3

Stood for parliament for three different parties:

Humphry Berkeley, Conservative MP for Lancaster 1959–66;

Labour candidate for North Fylde, October 1974; Social Democratic candidate for Southend East 1987

John Horam, Labour MP for Gateshead West 1970–81; Social Democrat MP for Gateshead West 1981–3; Conservative MP for Orpington from 1992. He was also parliamentary front bench spokesman for all three parties.

People's Parties:

Eelam People's Revolutionary Liberation Front; Sri Lanka

Ethiopian People's Revolutionary Democratic Front; Ethiopia

Flemish People's Union; Belgium

National People's Rally; UK

Pakistan People's Party; Pakistan

People's Action Party; Singapore

People's Alliance; Iceland

People's Democratic Movement; Turks and Caicos Islands

People's Democratic Union; Mali

People's National Party; Jamaica, Turks and Caicos Islands

People's Party; Austria

People's Progressive Party; Gambia

People's United Party; Belize

Rassemblement du Peuple Togolais; Togo

Swedish People's Party; Finland

The typical British Conservative:

70 per cent own stocks and shares

72 per cent bought shares in privatized industries

51 per cent have household incomes between £10,001 and £30,000

64 per cent left school at the age of 16 or earlier

89 per cent read a daily newspaper, but 94 per cent do not read *The Times*

88 per cent of Conservative voters under the age of 25 are not party members

VOTE FOR ME

Before a person can become an active politician, as opposed to one of the great mass of spectators in this greatest of all pastimes, he (or she, to be politically correct) has to find several people to vote for him (or her, still politically correct). Persuading the public actually to express a preference for one politician or another is the most difficult aspect of politics. Perhaps that is why Lord Butler, the 'greatest Prime Minister we never had', or at least one of the many great Prime Ministers we never had, described politics as 'the art of the possible'. If it is possible to persuade enough people to vote you on to the pitch to play the game, then anything is possible. It breeds confidence among those of us who have never stood for political office that crooks like Horatio Bottomley and Robert Maxwell can be elected from time to time with no hint of underhand dealings in the vote, that pornographic film stars like 'La Cicciolina' can persuade the Italian public that they are worthy public representatives, and that even spending vast sums of money cannot guarantee the public's affection, at least not for Michael Huffington, who spent over $25 million of his Texas oil fortune failing to be elected to the US Senate in 1994. His opponent, the incumbent Dianne Feinstein, spent over $14 million in protecting her seat, making it the first $40

million Senate race in history. Feinstein polled 3,593,069 votes, at a cost of about $3.90 per vote. Huffington's 3,481,840 votes cost him at least $7.20 each. Even Ross Perot's votes in the 1992 presidential election had not been that expensive, although Perot, worth around $3 billion, is possibly the richest man ever to run for democratic office anywhere in the world. Compare this with the £54 total outlay by James Maxton, the firebrand Clydesider Socialist, to be elected as an MP in the 1935 general election.

Ninety-eight years earlier, in 1896, the Republican Party sent out a total of 300 million election leaflets in support of their McKinley/Hobart ticket, enough for four copies for every man woman and child in America at the time. It worked. McKinley and Hobart won, with over seven million votes (one for every 43 leaflets used), handing the Democrat William Jennings Bryan the first of his three defeats in presidential elections.

The days are now long gone when a man could find a rotten borough to represent without having to worry about his electorate. Lord Palmerston, later a great Victorian Prime

Minister, was able to enter Parliament in 1807 as member for Newtown, Isle of Wight, on condition that he never visited the constituency, even when up for election. The proprietor of the rotten borough was worried that if he did visit the place, the voters might transfer their allegiance to Palmerston. There are probably many today who would vote for anybody who promised never to visit the constituency, never to hold election rallies, never to drive a loudspeaker van down the High Street, and never to write an asinine column in the local paper. But that is too much to hope for in these politically enlightened days.

Some politicians are more efficient than others in getting the votes. John Major, Prime Minister since 1990, became in 1992 the first Prime Minister since universal suffrage to have the largest majority of any government MP in the House of Commons. Major managed this by fair if occasionally eccentric means, which included standing on a rather flimsy soapbox to harangue the crowds around his constituency and elsewhere. Not all elections have been quite so scrupulously fair, and in some cases the fraud has been even greater than the one pointed out by a correspondent to Ann Landers, the American agony aunt, who complained that her husband had hidden her dentures on election day, so that she could not go out and vote Democrat.

There seems little doubt that Mayor Daley of Chicago delivered extra votes to the Democratic cause in the presidential election of 1960, which helped John F. Kennedy win Illinois by a mere 8,858 votes, fewer than the number of votes cast for a third candidate from the Socialist Labor Party. Nixon got fewer votes in Illinois eight years later, when he nevertheless carried the state. However, minor examples like this of creative vote-counting pale into insignificance beside the efforts of President Charles King of Liberia, who won the 1927 presidential election with a majority of 234,000. This is nothing when compared with the more than seven million votes majority that George Bush piled up over Michael Dukakis in the 1988 US presidential race, or the 5,800,000 lead that Bill Clinton had over Bush in 1992, but Liberia is a smaller country than the United States, and such vast majorities are unexpected. In 1927, after all, the vote in Liberia was restricted to 'male property owners of negro blood', of whom there were barely 15,000 in the entire country. The extent of President King's fraud was such that if Mr Clinton had attempted a vote-rigging exercise on a similar scale, he would have had a majority of almost 2.9 billion, almost three times the population of China, and over ten times the population of the United States. King's opponent, Thomas Faulkner, did not object to the result.

Voting in Communist countries was always decided beforehand by the Politburo rather than by the people at the ballot-box, but at least by the time that Communism collapsed, the

Soviet Union were getting quite good at making the results look half-way believable. Not so in North Korea, where the great leader Kim Il Sung's Workers' Party Of Korea took 100 per cent of the vote in a 100 per cent turn-out on 8 October 1962. In June of the same year, the Albanian Party of Labour (prop.: Enver Hoxha) persuaded all but seven of the voting population of 889,875 to go to the polls, and such was the strength of their political argument that all but 40 of the 889,868 who voted, voted for the Albanian Party of Labour. Luckily, it was a secret ballot, or those 40 who disagreed with the official view that Hoxha was the greatest political leader that any country had ever had might have been in trouble. By 1982, however, the Albanian Party of Labour ensured that the electorate was even more unanimous. The number of people eligible to vote had soared to 1,627,968, about half the population, and they all made it to the polling booths. Just one very brave or very stupid person decided not to vote for the only candidates available (all from the Albanian Party of Labour), giving the government a majority of 1,627,966 (99.99988 per cent of votes cast).

Large majorities have been won more legitimately by Boris Yeltsin (4,726,112 majority in Moscow, 1989: 89.4 per cent of votes cast), by HH the Maharani of Jaipur (157,692 majority in February 1962: 90.9 per cent of votes cast) and by Benazir Bhutto (80,250 majority in Larkana-III at the 1988 Pakistan general election: 96.7 per cent of votes cast). Louis-Adolphe Thiers was elected to the French National Assembly in 1870 by no fewer than 26 different *départements*, with a total vote of about one million, a huge proportion of the total potential electorate. The biggest majority ever won by a British politician is 120,247 by Mrs Glenys Kinnock (Labour) in the South Wales East constituency for the European elections in June 1994. This represented a 61.4 per cent majority of those who turned out to vote, but as only 43 per cent bothered to vote, Mrs Kinnock's actual vote represented just 32 per cent of the total electorate.

However, her victory was fairly and decisively won. In the same election, the far less runaway winner in the Kent East constituency (geographically the closest to the rest of Europe) was Mark Watts, whose majority was 635 votes, just 0.3 per cent of the votes cast. He actually gained only 34.6 per cent of the votes in a 40.3 per cent turn-out, so he received just under 14 per cent of the total votes of the potential electorate, and his majority was just over 0.1 per cent. The Conservatives, who came second, can hardly complain. Nineteen of mainland Britain's 84 MEPs were elected with less than 40 per cent of the votes cast in their favour, and of these 15 were Conservatives. Electoral reform will not feature very highly on the government's agenda if their European members have anything to do with it. There have so far been four European elections in which Britain has taken part, and never has the turn-out exceeded 40 per cent nationally. Even in Belgium, where voting is compulsory, the turn-out seems to stick around 93 per cent. The European Parliament fails to excite even the Belgians.

If we are looking for close elections, however, then we need look no farther than Zanzibar (which is quite far enough, I suppose). In their election of 1961 the Afro-Shirazi Party won control of Parliament by a single seat. That one seat was in the constituency of Chake Chake on Pemba Island, which they won by a single vote. In 1876, Rutherford Hayes received 250,000 fewer popular votes in the US presidential election than his Democratic opponent Samuel Tilden, but there was a dispute about the vote in the 'carpetbagger' states of Louisiana, South Carolina and Florida. An electoral commission was formed, which had a majority of Republicans. They voted strictly along party lines, and Hayes was elected by just one electoral vote. Tilden accepted the decision to avoid the possibility of rioting.

Hayes's successor, James Garfield, clocked up just 7,023 more votes in 1880 than Winfield Scott Hancock, a winning popular margin of just 0.16 per cent, but he had a majority of 59 electors in the College. Garfield had been chosen as the Republican nominee on the 36th ballot at the convention, beating President Grant, who otherwise would have been nominated for a third term as President. In 1884 Grover Cleveland carried New York State by a mere 1,100 votes, and with it the presidency, but four years later he lost to Benjamin Harrison despite winning almost 100,000 more votes. That was the last time that a President was elected with a smaller share of the popular vote than the loser. The biggest ever popular vote in a presidential election was given to Ronald Reagan, with 54,281,858 votes on his re-election in 1984, 100 years after Cleveland's victory. Reagan also won 525 electoral votes, beating by just two votes the previous record set by Franklin Delano Roosevelt in 1936.

Possibly the greatest political turnaround in democratic parliamentary history occurred on 24 October 1993, when Canadian voters threw out the Progressive Conservatives, led by the first woman Prime Minister of Canada, Mrs Kim

Campbell. Before the election, the Conservatives held 157 of the 295 seats in Parliament. After the votes were counted, they held just two, neither of which was Mrs Campbell's. After 125 years as one of the two great parties of Canadian politics, the Progressive Conservatives did not even secure the 12 seats required to qualify them for future federal funding. In the 1984 Canadian election the Liberals, who came out on top in 1993, had slumped from 147 seats to just 40, so dramatic swings are not unheard of north of the 49th parallel. However, the Progressive Conservatives have a long uphill battle to win back voter trust in Canada.

One of the key elements in winning votes is to have a great campaign slogan. If you can summarize your political ideals in a few words, and repeat these words often enough and convincingly enough between bouts of hand shaking and baby kissing, you are well on the way to a victory. The British Conservative Party in recent years have used slogans which tend to point out the deficiencies of their opponents rather than to promote their own virtues, such as the infamous

but brilliant 'Labour Isn't Working', with a photograph of a long queue of people waiting for the Job Centre to open. Macmillan's much lampooned 'You've Never Had It So Good' 20 years earlier was actually never said by him nor used by the Conservative Party, but it still passed into popular legend, and certainly worked in 1959. By 1964 the words 'never' and 'so good' had been deleted by the Labour Party, to give the electorate their slogan. John Major has tried 'Back to Basics', but the usual political trick of not defining terms has for once been seized upon by the media, with the result that the Conservatives have got caught up in unproductive explanations of which basics they feel we should all be getting back to, rather than just letting a snappy slogan rest against the backdrop of political in-fighting.

Some of the more adventurous campaign slogans have been born in the United States. There was 'Let Us Have Peace', which Theodore Roosevelt used to such effect that he subsequently won the Nobel Prize for Peace, and 'A Full Dinner Pail', which Chester Arthur used to little effect. Perhaps if he had not used the word 'pail', which implies his supporters did not have the most elegant of table manners, he might have done better. Teddy Roosevelt spoke of a 'Square Deal', which could conceivably have been a misprint for a 'square meal', a more socially acceptable version of Arthur's full dinner pail. In 1908 travelling salesmen across America wore buttons bearing the legend, 'Commercial Travellers For Taft'. Taft had often said, 'I'm something of a travelling man myself', and with the votes of the travelling salesmen (those who were not at the time entangled with the farmer's daughter), he inflicted a third defeat on the luckless William Jennings Bryan.

Woodrow Wilson's 1912 campaign sold buttons which read 'I am for Wilson and an Eight Hour Day', an election promise which unsurprisingly turned big business against him, but enabled him to win the day against his two predecessors, Teddy Roosevelt and William H. Taft. This was the only election in which two Presidents were beaten by a third candidate, who thus became President himself. Four years later, Wilson's supporters proclaimed 'He Kept Us Out Of The War', and his 'New Freedom' was for all. Within a year, Wilson took America into the war. Calvin Coolidge used the phrase 'Back To Normalcy' in 1924, coining not only a phrase but a new word, which has now entered the standard English dictionary and Lady Thatcher's memoirs. By 1928, however, 'normalcy' had disappeared to such an extent that he announced that he would not seek re-election. Franklin Roosevelt talked of a 'New Deal' and Kennedy of a 'New Frontier'. Lyndon Johnson searched for a 'Great Society'. When the writer Norman Mailer ran for the Democratic Party's nomination for Mayor of New York in 1969, he used the endearing slogan, 'No More Bullshit'.

This proved to be too radical a message for the citizens of New York, and he failed to win the nomination.

When Horatio Seymour, Governor of New York, campaigned as Democratic nominee for President against General Ulysses S. Grant in 1868 (just three years after Abraham Lincoln's assassination), his campaign song began with the couplet, 'Here's to the man that pulled the trigger/That killed the old cuss that freed the nigger.' Seymour was not elected.

Campaigning has changed completely in the past century. The electronic media have allowed every candidate's message to be heard by more people more quickly than ever before, but the politician still has to persuade the voters to put their cross in the right place on the ballot-paper. Some countries, such as Australia and Belgium, have chosen to make voting compulsory, but this only ensures that a mark is placed somewhere on the ballot-paper, not that it is placed against the name of the government candidate. In Ecuador they tried to eliminate many of the mistakes which can occur when an inexperienced voter enters the polling booth by passing a law in 1980 which made voting compulsory for all literate citizens over the age of 18, but voluntary for the illiterate ones (12 per cent of the adult population). Those who can do no more than mark an 'X' on the ballot-paper are thus excused even that.

Being able to read is not always enough. Interpreting what you read can be an equally important skill in some elections. When Roy Jenkins stood as SDP candidate at the Glasgow Hillhead by-election in March 1982, another candidate changed his name by deed poll to Roy Jenkins, creating confusion on the ballot paper which the original Mr Jenkins's supporters tried to overcome by standing outside the polling booths and indicating to voters as they arrived which of the two Roys was the SDP Roy. The voters of Glasgow Hillhead, whether deliberately or not, elected the original and not the impostor. When a man called Colin Hanoman tried to change his name to Margaret Thatcher to stand against the then Prime Minister in the 1983 general election, he was refused permission by the High Court and found himself stuck with his original name and a large legal bill. He did not run against Mrs Thatcher, although ten others did. Even so, Mrs Thatcher won more than half the votes cast.

Being allowed to cast a vote in the first place is the basic right that every democracy grants its citizens, or at least those citizens who fulfil certain criteria. Until the turn of the century, there were few nations which allowed their womenfolk a vote, or their men below the age of 25, or who did not possess property. The first country to allow the weaker sex to have a say in the political process was the Isle of Man, which opened the door to female suffrage in 1881. The American state of Wyoming had given women the vote in 1869, perhaps because there cannot have been many women in Wyoming in those frontier days. The initiative of the legislators of Wyoming, the final state alphabetically and the 49th out of 50 in population terms, was truly revolutionary, coming as it did only four years after slavery was abolished in the United States and just two years after Disraeli's Reform Bill had passed through the Mother of Parliaments and the cradle of parliamentary democracy. Disraeli's bill enfranchised the British 'working classes', giving the vote to as many as 27 per cent of the adult male population. It was not until 1889, 20 years after Wyoming had lived up to its official nickname of 'The Equality State', that Emmeline Pankhurst founded the Women's Franchise League in Britain.

Neither Wyoming nor the Isle of Man is an independent nation, of course, although the Isle of Man's own parliament, the Tynwald, has been in existence since the year AD979. Astonishingly, it seems that the cause of women's suffrage has been led by the British Empire, although Britain itself did not allow women the vote until after the First World War. In New Zealand, then still a colony, women were given the vote in 1893, and even the Australians, never famous for their liberal attitudes towards their womenfolk, granted them the vote in 1902. By the 1920s most nations had universal suffrage, although women did not get the vote in Japan, Italy or France until 1945. Switzerland held out until 1971, Jordan until 1973 and Liechtenstein until 1984.

It would be wrong to suggest that women did not have any say in the political process before they were granted the vote. Merely putting your cross against a name on a ballot-paper does not give a person any significant political influence. Miss

Emily Davison, the suffragette who threw herself to her death beneath the hooves of King George's horse Anmer in the 1913 Derby, was prepared to give her life to a cause which has changed the way we are all governed, and probably for the better. She and her fellow campaigners, like the suffragette who in 1908 got on to the floor of the House of Commons while it was in session and made even more noise than the politicians in mid-debate, did more without the vote than the vast majority of fully enfranchised women have done since. And it is interesting to note that at the 1900 general election, possibly the last one at which votes for women was not a central issue, 243 of the 670 members elected were returned without a contest. They stood unopposed, which effectively meant that not only all the women but also over one-third of male voters were effectively disenfranchised. During this century, the number of unopposed elections has decreased massively, to the extent that it became the custom that the Speaker of the House of Commons, who is non-partisan, was the only person who stood unopposed for election. But these days even that political courtesy has died and Speakers have to win election along with the rest of the members of the House of Commons. In America, Speakers have always had to fight their seats, but in 1994, in the wake of a political avalanche in favour of the Republicans, House Speaker Tom Foley became the first Speaker to lose his seat since 1860. Nevertheless, over 30 of the Congressmen returned in 1994 were returned unopposed, including 11 of the 23 Congressmen from Florida.

Sixteen women stood for election in the general election of 1918, including the leading suffragette, Christabel Pankhurst. This was the election at which more seats were contested –

707 – than ever before or since, and at which the turn-out was the lowest of the century. Only 59 per cent of the electorate, which had all but trebled since the previous election in 1910, bothered to vote, and they elected only one of the women who stood. She was an Irish Republican, Constance Georgina, Lady Markievicz, who was elected Sinn Fein member for Dublin City (St Patrick's), but never took up her seat at Westminster. Lady Markievicz was a daughter of Sir Henry Gore-Booth, a Sligo landowner, and she had been sentenced to death for her part in the 1916 Easter uprising, during which she shot, among other people, a Dublin society gentleman called Scovell. Mr Scovell was sitting in his club when he found himself caught up in the crossfire of revolution. A stray bullet nicked him, and as he looked out of the window to see who the culprit might be, he saw Lady Markievicz, probably still with a rifle in her hand. Scovell immediately picked up the telephone and put a call through to the Gore-Booth estate. The phone was answered by Lady Markievicz's brother. 'Look here, Gore-Booth,' said the irate clubman. 'I demand an apology. Your sister has just shot me, and in our club.' There is no certainty that this is the act for which she was sentenced to death, but in any case the sentence was commuted, and she moved from bullet to ballot without conviction (except for malicious wounding, of course).

Lady Markievicz refused to take her seat in the Commons because she regarded herself as Irish, and was fighting for a separate Irish state. Her leader in this struggle, Eamon De Valera, was another person who knew at first hand that women could sway the course of political events without having to resort to the vote. De Valera, the American-born son of a

Spanish immigrant, was made President of Sinn Fein in 1917, at the age of 28, and was almost inevitably arrested for revolutionary activities by the British authorities, who locked him up in Lincoln gaol. In 1918 he was elected MP for East Clare, but was unable to take his seat at Westminster even if he had wanted to, being behind bars at the time. However, in February 1919 he escaped from Lincoln gaol, an event which caused 'much excitement and amusement'. The amusement lay in the fact that De Valera's escape had been made possible by 'two beguiling girls who used their good looks to help his escape', as an author of the 1930s coyly worded it. Voteless but not helpless, these two beguiling girls had played a major part in one of the most important political stories of the century, to the amusement of all but the Lincoln gaol authorities.

There are still in Britain certain classes of people who are not entitled to vote, most of them being lunatics or peers, or any combination of the two. Peers are not allowed to vote because they have their own house within Parliament, and therefore have the right to take a far larger role in the government of the nation than ordinary untitled citizens. Lunatics are not allowed to vote, presumably to ensure that no more of their kind get elected than usual. In India a further class of citizen was finally granted the vote, in December 1994. Eunuchs, officially referred to as 'the third sex', had never been allowed to vote in India's elections, despite the fact that there were over 5,000 of them in Delhi alone, perhaps on the grounds that there would be no future generations to complain of this injustice. What has not been explained is whether all Indian males had to take a medical examination before entering the polling station, to check whether or not they were entitled to vote. The activities of most British, French and American politicians seem to show that there are no physical eunuchs among them, whatever their philosophical qualities when it comes to creating new ideas and policies.

In most democracies, voting only takes place once every four or five years, so for most of the time, keen voters are deprived of the joys of standing in a booth in a deserted school assembly hall or village community centre, marking a ballot-paper in favour of somebody they know almost nothing about. But occasionally, there is an event of sufficient moment to require a further specific choice to be made by the voters, and at these times there is public outcry for a referendum. A referendum is a vote on a single issue which for some reason the national government does not feel it should make itself, despite the fact that the nation, earnestly desiring not to have to take political decisions more often than is strictly required, has elected members of parliament to take these decisions for them. Membership of the European Union is perhaps the most obvious example of a basis for a referendum, but other issues, from capital punishment to taxation, have been suggested by proponents of the referendum as something to keep the professional politicians on their toes. The great difference between a referendum and an election is that whereas an election is on the whole a fair test of popularity, a referendum is not.

The only referendum ever held in Britain was in 1975, when the question asked was 'Do you think the United Kingdom should stay in the European Community (Common Market)? YES/NO.' This looks like a very open question, but actually pollsters could show that people tend to want to say YES when the option is there. As we shall see, a fairer question would have been along the lines of 'Do you think the United Kingdom should stay in the European Community or get out?' Several other countries' parliaments have asked their electorate to make this particular decision for them, but none quite as brazenly as the Danes, who discovered that the post-Maastricht electorate wanted to leave the EU when the referendum votes were all counted, so the government

called another referendum. This is the kind of underhand tactic which the Green Party in Brazil, for one, is so against. They fought their 1994 election with several million sheets of literature to woo the voters to their ecological cause. After the election, they put all the unused papers into a recycling process, in the best traditions of saving the planet. Unfortunately for them, the election was inconclusive and had to be re-run, but the Greens could not afford to reprint all their literature. They failed to do as well the second time around.

The second Danish referendum was won by the pro-Europe lobby, but despite protests from the anti-Europeans, the government turned down the idea of a deciding referendum, to make it a 'best of three' series, and have decided to keep the country within Europe, whether the electorate want it or not. The Swedes voted narrowly to go into Europe in 1994, but the Norwegians voted to stay out. The referendum is a dangerous weapon which can strike down those who thought it would defend them.

And consider the different ways there are of asking the same question. 'Should Britain be in the Common Market?' is a simple yes/no question, but what if it is phrased thus: 'Do you want Great Britain to remain an independent state?' Or thus: 'Do you wish any further powers hitherto exercised by the British Parliament to be transferred to an unelected polyglot junta sitting in a foreign capital?' The first alternative (suggested by the UK Independence Party) assumes that Great Britain is currently 'an independent state', independent of economic and trading decisions made around the world by competitors and customers alike, and that continuing in Europe would somehow further erode that independence. It is, of course, possible that the UK Independence Party's point of view is entirely correct, but the fact that this viewpoint is hidden behind the words of the question is what makes it a dangerous question. The second alternative, suggested by the socialist Lord Stoddart of Swindon, of the Campaign For An Independent Britain, is obviously biased against those members of the 'unelected polyglot junta' in Brussels, but the problems with the question are that, firstly it is not at all straightforward in its use of language, and secondly that the answer 'yes' is not the one that the organizers want to hear. Rule number one in phrasing a referendum question is to make sure that the answer you want is 'yes', because people are naturally more inclined, by up to eight percentage points according to some statistical surveys, to say 'yes' than 'no'.

If voting is a potential minefield, why not just use a minefield? There is a more pleasant option, at least for the candidate, than having to win votes, and that is to take power in a military coup. Between 1825, when Bolivia became a sovereign country on gaining its independence from Spain, and 1990, statisticians have calculated that there have been almost 200 *coups d'état* in Bolivia. The large number explains the need for statisticians rather than historians to be consulted; the uncertainty over the total is because only 23 of the attempted coups have actually succeeded, and some of the unsuccessful ones have been put down to military over-exuberance rather than the use of political force. Bolivia began with a Venezuelan 'Life President', one Antonio José Sucré, but he was overthrown after only two years in office. That proved to be one of the longer stays in power in La Paz.

A much more original coup occurred in 1993, across the

Atlantic Ocean from Bolivia, when President Bantubonke Holomisa of Transkei, one of the old South African 'homelands', effectively overthrew himself by abolishing his country and reuniting it with South Africa. That's certainly one way of retiring from politics.

SUPPLEMENTARIES

Small votes

0 votes: Mr Wideon Pyfrom, Free National Party, Rolleville, Bahamas, July 1977

5 votes: Commander W. Boaks, Public Safety Democratic Monarchist White Resident Party, Glasgow Hillhead by-election, March 1982

5 votes: Dr Kailish Trevedi, Independent Janata Party, Kensington by-election, July 1988

7 votes: J. Connell, Peace Party, Chesterfield by-election, March 1984

8 votes: Esmond Bevan, Independent, Bermondsey by-election, February 1983

10 votes: Peter Reed Smith, Republican, Darlington by-election, March 1983

At British elections, a candidate has to obtain the signatures of ten voters within the constituency before being able to stand. To get fewer than ten votes on election day is therefore something of an achievement.

Low share of popular vote for a man elected President:

Abraham Lincoln, 1860, 39.8%

Woodrow Wilson, 1912, 41.9%

Political slogans:

'In Your Heart You Know He's Right' – Republican slogan at 1964 election

'A Land Fit for Heroes to Live in' – Coalition slogan at 1918 general election

'Lords Versus the People' – Liberal slogan at 1910 general election

'Peace and Bread' – Bolshevik slogan during the 1917 revolution

'Safety First' – Conservative slogan at 1929 general election

'Socialism in Our Time' – Labour slogan at 1929 general election

'Tranquillity' – Conservative slogan at 1922 general election (described by Lloyd George as 'not a policy, but a yawn')

'Trial of the Kaiser; Punishment of those responsible for Atrocities; the Fullest Indemnities from Germany until the Lemon Pips Squeak; Britain for the British Socially and Industrially; Rehabilitation for those Broken in the War, and a Happier Country for All' – slogan at 1918 general election

'Who Governs Britain?' – Conservative slogan at 1974 general election

'You Know Labour Government Works' – Labour slogan at 1966 general election

3 POLITICAL LEADERS AND POLITICAL OFFICE

What makes a national leader? What is the difference between, say, Harry S Truman, President of the United States for eight years, and William Jennings Bryan, three times an unsuccessful Democratic nominee for President? How come the history books will devote chapters to the career of Margaret Thatcher, while Michael Foot will be little more than the occupant of a minor paragraph? What did Stalin have that Beria did not? How did Boris Yeltsin so easily dispose of Mikhail Gorbachev and what were the main reasons for Mitterrand's triumph over Giscard d'Estaing? Can we define the characteristics of a successful national leader, one for whom the people will vote despite, rather than because of, their political ideals and their party's policies?

There are many factors which make a leader acceptable to the people. Brute force combined with terror often works to persuade citizens that they are led by a truly glorious leader, but this tactic will not often survive the ballot-box. Age is a factor in some societies: in general the older leaders come from the countries which do not have a Christian tradition. Respect for age is a Confucian virtue, not a WASP one. Gender is also a factor, as most societies are still wary of choosing a female leader, despite the undoubted strengths and electability of such as Indira Gandhi, Golda Meir and Margaret Thatcher. Perhaps Kim Campbell and Edith Cresson have set the cause of female leaders back in recent years, but once the Australians elect a woman as Prime Minister, we will know that the sexual barricades in politics have finally collapsed.

The political ideals of a leader seem to make very little difference to his (or her) chances of success with the electorate. The national and indeed global mood seems to swing a little from left to right and back again, but in general one cannot say that a Democrat is more voter friendly than a Republican or that a Socialist is more psephologically challenged than a Conservative. Even the most astute political commentators find it very difficult to tell the difference between a right-wing Socialist, a left-of-centre Conservative and a pragmatic Liberal Democrat, anyway, so what chance is there for the average voter? Policies very rarely dominate elections: national moods and the degree of confidence the different party leaders inspire among the voting public are the more important factors. I would suggest, however, that being a self-confessed cannibal cannot be good for one's electoral chances. Dr Roberto Canessa,

one of 16 survivors of an air crash in the Andes in 1972 who survived ten weeks in the snows by eating those of their fellow passengers who had been killed and who looked chewy, stood for the presidency of Uruguay in 1994. We may never know whether it was his internationally renowned bout of cannibalism, the subject of a best-selling book and a big budget film, or his policies which let him down, but anyway, he was not elected.

The media manipulate carefully, but even they cannot guarantee the success of their favourites. Yet there is one factor that seems to rise above political dogma, above the national mood and beyond media manipulation, one factor that can help us to identify the winner of an election before it is held. It is a factor that only one major election in recent years has failed to confirm, when the Canadian general election of 1993 threw out the Progressive Conservatives (a title which is in itself a wonderful contradiction in terms) led by Mrs Kim Campbell, and elected the Liberal Jean Chrétien as Prime Minister.

Kim Campbell had far more than M. Chrétien of the one secret ingredient a national leader needs, a secret ingredient shared by John Major, Bill Clinton, Boris Yeltsin and even by François Mitterrand, at least in comparison with Giscard d'Estaing. The secret ingredient is hair. Forget your spin doctors, don't worry about political doctrine and ride untroubled over every sleazy scandal that besets your party. Just choose a leader with a fine head of hair, and look after it well. To this general truth, we can add one important rider – the hair must be on the top of the head, not elsewhere. Beards are bad political news, as Chancellor Kohl found to his delight in the August

1994 German elections when his main opposition, the Social Democrats, went into battle led by Rudolf Scharping, a man with far more hair on the top of his head than Herr Kohl, but – crucially – also a beard on his chin. The voters kept Kohl in by 0.3 per cent of the vote, 48.4 per cent to 48.1 per cent, despite the fact that 'Kohl' is the German for 'cabbage', making Germany the only major democracy led by a vegetable.

Consider the facts: successful American presidential candidates are always the hairiest on offer. Clinton's fine head of hair outdistanced George Bush and his more conservative locks. Bush himself previously had no difficulty against Michael Dukakis, possibly because Dan Quayle, his definitely not balding vice-presidential nominee, had far more hair than the Democratic vice-presidential candidate, the remarkably smooth-pated Senator Lloyd Bentsen. Ms Geraldine Ferraro, the only woman to be nominated for one of the top two slots by one of the major parties, failed, as running mate of Walter Mondale in 1980, to overcome Ronald Reagan, and his thick black locks. Before him, Jimmy Carter had wiped the floor with

Gerald Ford simply because he had more hair. Both men are left-handed, so it could not have been that that separated them in the voters' minds.

Nixon had no trouble against Humphrey, but no chance against Kennedy. Eisenhower was lucky enough to be up against Adlai Stevenson twice, one of the few men in America at the time with less hair than Ike, and so it goes on. In Britain, the Labour Party have persisted in choosing leaders who are thin on top, which has not helped their chances with the British voters. What chance had Neil Kinnock against John Major? Even Michael Foot, a man with hair as plentiful and as unruly as the Labour Party when he led them, was up against Margaret Thatcher, and so suffered the inevitable defeat. Edward Heath and Harold Wilson, men with roughly equal quantities of hair, swapped power during the 1970s, once the Conservatives had forfeited power by going into an election led by Sir Alec Douglas-Home. Before that it was Macmillan and Eden, whose hairstyles were more than a match for anything the Socialists could pit against them. What's more, they both had moustaches, which are not the kiss of death for the electorate in the way that full beards are, except in the United States. The most recent President with a moustache was William H. Taft, who presided over 80 years ago, from 1909 to 1913, and the moustache-ridden Thomas Dewey suffered a shock defeat at the hands of Truman in 1948.

Compare also Boris Yeltsin, with his fine shock of hair, with Mikhail Gorbachev. The first ever reasonably free election in Russia was won by the man with the best head of hair, although Russian political folk wisdom has it that their leaders are alternately hairy and bald. A bald man can always lead a country if he does not have to subject himself to popular election first, and Russia's baldies, from Lenin via Khrushchev and Andropov to Gorbachev, have done as much for their country as the hairier Stalin, Brezhnev and Chernenko. In Russian terms, bald heads are supposed to imply thoughtfulness, while a full head of hair shows a man governed by his emotions. But when the people have the choice, it seems they like a hairy man, even if he is emotional to boot. Compare Nelson Mandela with F. W. de Klerk. Look at Lech Walesa and General Jaruzelski. The party led by the person with the best head of hair wins every major election. I rest my case.

Given this undoubted political truth, it is not surprising that the pre-war Conservative Cabinet Minister Leslie Hore-Belisha took the precaution of wearing not only a hat but also a wig to cover his otherwise rather bald head. This caused him some difficulty when, in 1939, he became involved in an argument while staying at the Ritz Hotel in Paris. In the heat of the battle, his antagonist grabbed the wig and flushed it down the lavatory. Luckily there was an arrangement by which hotel staff could fish out valuable items as they passed through the plumbing system, but Hore-Belisha was not keen to place the wig back on his head immediately. He left the hotel covered in a rug, pleading a heavy cold, and the wig was returned by the diplomatic bag to Mr Hore-Belisha once it had been cleaned up, permed and made to smell like the best French scent. Mr Hore-Belisha, being a wig man rather than a genuinely hairy person, never made it to the position of party leader, but he did have those flashing beacons at pedestrian crossings named after him, an apt memorial for a bald man.

Milton Pitts, who died at the end of 1994, was described

by Henry Kissinger as 'a persistent foreign policy adviser and I liked him a lot', but more importantly, Kissinger acknowledged that Pitts was 'a great barber'. Pitts was barber to four Republican Presidents, Nixon, Ford, Reagan and Bush. He charged $25 and took with him to his grave the secret of whether or not Ronald Reagan's hair was dyed. Of course, dyed hair is not a political issue, just as long as there is enough hair to dye. Bill Clinton, who abandoned Mr Pitts's salon in favour of the more fashionable Cristophe (sic), found that his elegantly coiffed hair-do, which had helped him reach the White House, was in danger of losing him popular support as well as money. Cristophe may well be a man who cannot spell his own name properly, but he knows how to charge for a haircut. His rates apparently started at $200, a sum that would have got him eight cuts at Milton Pitts's salon, but to be fair to him, he also seems to take about eight times as long. President Clinton kept Air Force One waiting on the tarmac at Los Angeles for a couple of hours in 1993 while Cristophe cut his rug, creating both a magnificent bouffant hairstyle and

air traffic chaos in Southern California. Analysts deemed the cut 'a political mistake and cultural myopia', but unless the Republicans can come up with a significantly hairier candidate in 1996, it may well be President Clinton who has the last laugh.

Similarly, political analysts in Britain know that John Major, who was a clear follicular leader when compared with Neil Kinnock and John Smith, still has the edge on Tony Blair, and provided the Conservative Party keeps its nerve up to the next general election, he should have a strong chance of presiding over yet another Tory victory. Nevertheless, it must be of some concern to the Conservatives that Mr Blair could cause a minor political scandal by spending £60 on a haircut, as he did late in 1994. If Mr Blair has enough hair to warrant spending £60 on, he must be a serious rival in any election within the next year or two. If the Conservatives lose their nerve and ditch Mr Major for somebody else before the next election, due by April 1997, they may well be in trouble, unless that somebody else is Virginia Bottomley, of course. Or Michael Portillo.

Dandruff, according to a report in *The Times* of 3 November 1994, is an occupational disease of politicians. Parliamentarians are for some reason statistically more likely to suffer from dandruff than most other sectors of the population. They are predominately male, of course, keep late hours in a muggy atmosphere and worry a lot (especially about their prospects of re-election), none of which is good for what is essentially a skin condition. Nevertheless, there are more votes in having a head of hair, even complete with dandruff, than in being bald. It matters not how thin the policies are, as long as the hair does not match. The only thing wrong with this particular political theory is that, by rights, Screaming Lord Sutch, the very hirsute leader of the Official Monster Raving Loony Party, should be Prime Minister, but perhaps his day will come.

I remember taking part several years ago in a debate (the ideal training ground for would-be politicians: I was never much good), where the motion was 'This House disapproves of long hair and all that goes with it.' The cause was won by an enterprising speaker, no doubt now at least a local councillor somewhere, who argued that what most often goes with long hair is a lady, and this House did not disapprove of women. Women have certainly had an uphill struggle to make their mark in politics, even as participants, let alone as leaders. As long ago as 1884 Mrs Belva Lockwood stood as the Equal Rights Party candidate in the US presidential election, but did not do well, mainly because women did not have the vote in America at the time. Since then, apart from Geraldine Ferraro, the only woman to have made a realistic bid for the presidency is the Republican Senator Margaret Chase Smith, who entered a few primaries in 1964, 'to point out that a lady candidate is a possibility'.

The first woman to become Prime Minister anywhere in the world was Mrs Sirimavo Bandaranaike, who took over the leadership of Sri Lanka's Freedom Party when her husband, Solomon Bandaranaike, was assassinated in 1959 by, of all unlikely people, a Buddhist monk. They became the first husband and wife ever both to become Prime Minister, and matters went a stage further when their daughter, Chandrika Bandaranaike Kumaratunga, became President of Sri Lanka in 1994. She then appointed her 78-year-old mother Prime Minister once again, making her span of premiership, at 35 years, one of the longest in the world. Mrs Bandaranaike is certainly the only person of either gender to have been appointed Prime Minister by her own daughter, reversing the usual generational inheritance in politics.

Leaders, once they get there, tend to try to stay in power. This is perhaps a natural desire, and all will agree who have climbed the greasy pole that staying there is no easier than the journey to the summit. Lots of things can combine to eliminate one from office: illness, the electorate, financial and sexual scandals, very occasionally voluntary retirement and, far more often, death. Getting to the top early helps to ensure a long stay in power, as Fidel Castro has found out in Cuba. Thirty-five years after he ousted General Batista at the age of 31, he is still head of state. Flight Lieutenant Jerry Rawlings (now President Rawlings) followed Castro's example in 1981 in Ghana, where he seized power at the age of 34. In Libya, Colonel Gaddafi was only 27 years old when he took power in 1969 and is still there 25 years later. In Haiti, Jean-Claude 'Baby Doc' Duvalier was only 19 years old when he succeeded his father as President for Life in 1971, but he lasted until 1986, becoming at the age of 34 probably one of the youngest ex-Presidents for Life ever known, and certainly one of the very few Presidents for Life to survive being overthrown. It remains to be seen whether Dr Mario Frick, who was democratically elected Prime Minister of the Principality of Liechtenstein in 1993 at the age of 28, will last as long as other less freely appointed young leaders. Confusingly, Dr Frick is remarkably bald despite his youth.

Generally speaking, if you wish to be a successful political leader, it is best to make the attempt in your own home country. The Americans even have a rule that a President must be born in the United States, which is why Andrew Jackson, the seventh President, made sure it was officially recorded that he was born on 15 March 1767 in South Carolina, the posthumous son of Andrew Jackson, who, like his wife Elizabeth, was an Irish immigrant. However, it is quite probable that he was actually born a couple of years earlier, in 1755, on board ship bound for the Carolinas, when his father was still alive. Britain has had one Prime Minister born in Canada, Andrew Bonar Law, and an MP, Edward Blake, who had previously been Leader of the Canadian Opposition. Blake gave up the leadership of the Canadian Liberal Party in 1891 and became Nationalist MP for South Longford at Westminster the following year. In more recent times Bryan Gould, a candidate for the British Labour Party leadership in 1992, was born in New Zealand.

Some people, however, have become leaders of more than one country, and not only by the Napoleonic or Hitlerian method of acquiring by force of arms more countries to be leader of. Several leaders have changed the names of the country they lead, of course, but this does not count as leading two nations. Ceylon and Sri Lanka are the same geographical unit, as are Burma and Myanmar, and the Gold Coast and Ghana. Much more versatile than the leaders of these renamed nations is Eduard Shevardnadze, who was for some years the Foreign Minister of the Soviet Union. By the end of 1992, he was President of Georgia. Che Guevara, an Argentine by birth, rose to political prominence in Cuba and died leading a guerrilla uprising in Bolivia. It is US President Taft, however, who tops them all. Before being elected President in 1908, he was

Governor of the Philippines from 1901 to 1904, and provisional Governor of Cuba in 1906. After his presidential term, he became Chief Justice of the United States, and remains the only man to have been chief executive of three nations, as well as the only man to have headed both the judicial and executive parts of the US Government.

Leaders, whether of one or several countries, are not always very good at recognizing each other. James Callaghan, when Prime Minister of Britain, hosted a dinner during the NATO Summit meeting in London in May 1977, at which he announced that General Ramalho Eanes, then President of Portugal, Britain's oldest military ally, was 'a worthy representative of the new democracy in Brazil'. Two years earlier, Gerald Ford had toasted President Sadat of Egypt with the words, 'To you and the people you represent, the great people of the government of Israel.' Ronald Reagan forgot which country he was in during a whistle-stop tour of South America, but it was President George Bush who committed the ultimate *faux pas* at the dinner table, by falling off his chair and throwing up over his host, the Japanese Prime Minister, during an official dinner in Tokyo.

Is there money in being a political leader? If you are Prime Minister of Japan, there certainly is. His annual salary

in 1994 reached ¥38,463,360 including monthly allowances and bonuses, which is about £235,000, although job security is not particularly good. It is also unclear exactly how the bonuses work. Japanese members of both the upper and lower chambers of the Diet receive ¥23,633,565 (about £145,000) in salary, although perks, share option schemes and the contents of unmarked envelopes tend to inflate these salary levels significantly. The President of the United States is currently on $200,000 a year, plus expenses, and the Vice-President is paid $171,500 a year plus expenses. Not bad for a job which involves sitting in an outer office waiting to hear the President sneeze, a job which John Nance Garner, FDR's Vice-President from 1933 to 1941, described as 'not worth a pitcher of spit'. Pitchers of spit are obviously getting quite expensive.

Most nations are torn between paying enough to attract the best people into politics and not paying so much that every villain in the capital heads for the parliament building like jackals to a rotting corpse. The British Prime Minister earns £78,292, which is £42,000 less than the Lord Chancellor earns, but prime ministerial memoirs earn more than a mere Lord Chancellor's, so in the long run, the Prime Minister does not do too badly. American cabinet members (unelected, it should be remembered) earn $148,400, half as much again as their British counterparts on £64,749. But power rather than money is what attracts people into the political process, and the best politicians are part villain, anyway. The most effective Presidents in recent years have been Lyndon Johnson and Richard Nixon, neither of whom one would have trusted with 50 pence for a loaf of bread, but who as leaders knew how to win. The nice guys, like Jimmy Carter and George Bush, fail to win re-election. Saints are not good political leaders, even if they come cheap. George Lansbury, the British Labour Party leader of the 1930s, was described by one of his fellow MPs as 'so good, he'll have us all in heaven before our time'. A fine man and a committed Christian, Lansbury would have been a disastrous national leader, which fortunately the people of Britain recognized: although as the alternative was Neville Chamberlain, perhaps Lansbury could not have done much worse.

There is no country which pays its politicians nothing, although Britain paid its MPs nothing until 1911, and George Washington set a fine precedent when he fought the War of Independence on expenses. Items like 'food for one army' have been found in his papers, which must have compensated for the fact that he received no salary. If a President or a Prime Minister today could claim for 'food for one Cabinet', Cabinet meetings would last rather longer, and promotion to the Cabinet would depend on your eating habits rather than your political strengths. And Dr Roberto Canessa would never be in anybody's cabinet.

SUPPLEMENTARIES

Women who have led their countries:

Mrs Corazon Aquino, President of the Philippines, 1986–92

Mrs Sirimavo Bandaranaike, Prime Minister of Ceylon (later Sri Lanka) 1960–65, 1970–77, 1994

Hon. Benazir Bhutto, Prime Minister of Pakistan, 1988–90 and from 1993

Mrs Kim Campbell, Prime Minister of Canada, 1993

Mrs Mary E. Charles, Prime Minister of Dominica, from 1980

Ms Tansu Ciller, Prime Minister of Turkey, from 1994

Mme Edith Cresson, Prime Minister of France, 1991–2

Mrs Vigdis Finnbogadottir, President of Iceland, from 1980

Mrs Indira Gandhi, Prime Minister of India, 1966–77, 1980–84

Mrs Chandrika Bandaranaike Kumaratunga, President of Sri Lanka, 1994

Mrs Golda Meir, Prime Minister of Israel, 1969–74

Mrs Maria Estela Perón, President of Argentina, 1974–5

Dr Maria Lurdes Pintasilgo, Prime Minister of Portugal, August to November 1979

Mrs Mary Robinson, President of Ireland, from 1990

Mrs Margaret Thatcher, Prime Minister of the UK, 1979–90

Begum Khaleda Zia, Prime Minister of Bangladesh, from 1991

Women on the ballot for the presidential election, 1992:

Lenora Fulani (New Alliance), 73,248 votes

Helen Halyard (Workers' League), 3,050 votes

Isabelle Masters (Looking Back Group), 327 votes

Gloria Estella La Riva (Workers' World), 181 votes

Vice-Presidents of the USA who became President by election rather than through succession by death or resignation:

John Adams, 1797

Thomas Jefferson, 1801

Martin Van Buren, 1837

Richard M. Nixon, 1969

George Bush, 1989

George Bush was the first current Vice-President to run successfully for President for 152 years.

Two-term Vice-Presidents of the USA:

John Adams (1789–97), Vice-President to George Washington

George Clinton (1805–12), Vice-President to Thomas Jefferson and James Madison, died in office 20 April 1812

Daniel D. Tompkins (1817–25), Vice-President to James Monroe

John C. Calhoun (1825–32), Vice-President to John Quincy Adams and Andrew Jackson, resigned 28 December 1832 on election to the Senate

Thomas R. Marshall (1913–21), Vice-President to Woodrow Wilson

John Nance Garner (1933–41), Vice-President to Franklin D. Roosevelt

Richard M. Nixon (1953–61), Vice-President to Dwight D. Eisenhower

Spiro T. Agnew (1969–73), Vice-President to Richard M. Nixon, resigned 10 October 1973, within a year of re-election

George Bush (1981–9), Vice-President to Ronald Reagan

Four Vice-Presidents within four years:

Spiro T. Agnew, resigned 10 October 1973

Gerald R. Ford, 10 October 1973 until assumed presidency 9 August 1974

Nelson A. Rockefeller, 9 August 1974 until end of term, January 1977

Walter F. Mondale, from 20 January 1977

Presidents who never had a Vice-President:

John Tyler (1841–5)

Millard Fillmore (1850–53)

Andrew Johnson (1861–5)

Chester A. Arthur (1881–5)

Vice-Presidents who became President through death of incumbent and then subsequently won Presidency in their own right:

Theodore Roosevelt, became President 14 September 1901 on death of McKinley; won presidential election 1904

Calvin Coolidge, became President 3 August 1923 on death of Harding; won presidential election 1924

Harry S Truman, became President 12 April 1945 on death of F. D. Roosevelt; won presidential election 1948

Lyndon B. Johnson, became President 22 November 1963 on death of Kennedy; won presidential election 1964

Left-handed Presidents since the Second World War:

Harry S Truman, Gerald Ford, Jimmy Carter, George Bush, Bill Clinton

Right-handed Presidents since the SecondWorld War:

Dwight D. Eisenhower, John F. Kennedy, Lyndon B. Johnson, Richard M. Nixon, Ronald Reagan

Leaders of the British Labour Party who did not become Prime Minister:

James Keir Hardie, Arthur Henderson, George Lansbury, Hugh Gaitskell, Michael Foot, Neil Kinnock, John Smith

Leaders of the British Conservative Party who did not become Prime Minister:

None

First official use of the term 'Prime Minister':

In the Treaty of Berlin, 1878, which was signed by the newly ennobled Disraeli as 'Beaconsfield, First Lord of the Treasury and Prime Minister of Her Britannic Majesty'.

Three vice-presidential candidates in one party:

The Democrats in 1972 first nominated Senator Thomas Eagleton to run with Senator George McGovern. He dropped out after details of his mental illnesses were leaked. McGovern offered the place on the ticket to Senator Ed Muskie, who eventually turned it down. Third choice Sargent Shriver went down to defeat with McGovern.

THE POLITICAL PROCESS

Speeches by politicians too often read badly. There are exceptions, of course, but oratory is an oral, not a visual art. A quick read of the text of John Prescott's stirring speech at the Labour Party Conference in 1993, in support of John Smith's bid to sell to his own party the principle of one man one vote, will prove this to any doubters. The audience was on its feet to acclaim the forthright and convincing oratory of the one-time merchant navy bar steward, but when his actual words were reread in the bleak columns of the next morning's newspapers, it was easy to see that what Prescott actually said was a combination of bizarre grammar and complete nonsense. This combination is a winning one, though. All sorts of politicians in many different parties and many different countries use it to great effect.

Some politicians have been so pleased with their speeches that they have put them on record, enabling us to get the flavour of their style on the hustings. Gladstone, in 1888, was the first British Prime Minister to commit himself to wax. He recorded a cylinder on 22 November that year, but it was only as a favour to Thomas Edison, who had requested a record of Gladstone's voice. Count Otto von Bismarck also recorded his voice that same year. From the turn of the century, most

statesmen seized the chance to be immortalized on record, and there are recordings by Presidents Theodore Roosevelt, Taft, Wilson, Harding, Coolidge and Franklin Delano Roosevelt on file. Taft was the only one of these Presidents to use the record as an election tool, making over 40 cylinders during August 1908, just before his election.

Taft's 40 cylinders of speechifying is nothing when compared with the true masters of political long-windedness. Senator Wayne Morse of Oregon spoke for 22 hours and 26 minutes through 24 and 25 April 1953 on the Tidelands Oil Bill. He did not stop, yield the floor or pause for lunch. This feat was matched by Senator Strom Thurmond, then a South Carolina Democrat, who spoke for 24 hours and 19 minutes from 28 to 29 August 1957, except that he did give way briefly so that a new Senator could be sworn in. The new Senator must have wondered what sort of a madhouse he was entering.

The American tradition of filibustering does not, thankfully, find a counterpart in Britain. John Golding MP, then Labour MP for Newcastle-under-Lyme, spoke for 11 hours and 15 minutes in committee, on various small amendments to the British Telecommunications Bill in February 1983, but this is almost three times as long as anybody has ever spoken in a debate proper in the House of Commons. Ivan Lawrence QC MP (Conservative, Burton) spoke for 4 hours and 23 minutes when opposing the Water Fluoridization Bill on 6 March 1985, beating a record that had been held by Sir Bernard Braine (Conservative, Essex South East), who spoke for 3 hours and 16 minutes on 23 and 24 July 1974. Sir Bernard, who had stated before rising that he hoped to 'make the longest speech of this Parliament so far from the back benches', made his wish come true. He rose at 10.16 p.m. with the words, 'I rise to oppose the third reading of the British Railways Bill', the sort of opening gambit that can clear a chamber in seconds. The main thrust of his argument was that he actually opposed only one provision of the Bill, 'namely that which is contained in Clause Six which enables British Railways to construct a railway line and sidings to serve the oil refineries on Canvey Island'. To this end, he carried on until 1.33 a.m., filling 71 columns of *Hansard* in the process. Then the question was put, 'that the debate be now adjourned'. The voting was Ayes, nil: Noes, one (Sir Bernard). There being 39 fewer MPs present than a quorum (40), the business stood over.

The art of long speeches is not limited to British and American politicians, though. Fidel Castro spoke for 4½ hours to the United Nations on 26 September 1960, which was a long haul for his international audience, but which would have been seen as a few after-dinner remarks by his fellow Cubans, whom he has harangued many times for longer than a mere 4½ hours. Chief Mangosuthu Buthelezi, the Zulu leader, spoke to the

KwaZulu legislative assembly over an 18-day period from 12 to 29 March 1993. He spoke on 11 of the 18 days, for a total of about 27 hours, and nobody called him 'an old windbag', a term of abuse reluctantly allowed by the Speaker in the British Parliament. If he had been as rapid a speaker as Leslie Hale, the post-war Labour MP, who spoke at what was described as 'the unreportable rate' of 300 words a minute, or John F. Kennedy, who sometimes approached that speed, he probably would have finished his speech in a mere 10 days or so.

Some politicians speak as little as is possible without actually forfeiting the chance of getting re-elected. In any given year, there will be perhaps a dozen British MPs who say nothing whatsoever in the House, and a similar proportion of silent Senators, Deputies and Diet Members can be found in parliaments all around the world. These are the legislators who are much loved by Speakers, who never have to complain to them, as Mr Speaker did in the 1977 Abortion debate in the House of Commons: 'I strongly deprecate Hon. Members giving the assurance they will speak for only five minutes and then speaking for 22 minutes.' The legendary Captain Henry

Kerby, Conservative MP for Arundel and Shoreham from 1954 until his death on 4 January 1971, rarely spoke for even five minutes, let alone 22. He was reputed to have asked only three questions during his 17 years as a Member of Parliament. Two of these questions were written, and the third was 'Could somebody please open a window?' Unfortunately, research through the pages of *Hansard* showed that Captain Kerby, whom I well remember addressing a political meeting I attended as a schoolboy in 1964, did speak rather more often than legend has it, and asked several important written questions. He was not a major orator, and actually did not speak in Parliament for at least five consecutive years between 1961 and 1966 (during which time he won re-election twice), but he did speak in the debate on the Queen's Speech on 3 November 1960, on the subject of British East Africa, and again to intervene in the metrication debate of 27 October 1970. He was not a progressive thinker, however, and his views on metrication can be summed up in the closing words of his speech: 'No defence exists against this latest madness except for the nation itself to cry, "No! Stop!" and that in the voice of outrage, loud and clear.' He could have used those words to close practically all of his political speeches on any subject, and probably did. His views on racial harmony are encapsulated in his contribution to the Sales of Arms to South Africa debate in July 1970. The Labour Member Judith Hart referred to 'the policy of sanctions, which was supported by the honourable gentlemen opposite', at which Captain Kerby interjected, 'Not all!' And then he sat down and shut up for three months.

His written questions varied from asking the value of packets in four mailbags stolen from a Waterloo to Teddington train in March 1961 (answer: £616.17.11d) to the more usual concerns of shire Tories, as with his question of 17 July 1963 to the Lord Privy Seal, Edward Heath: 'How many members of the Foreign Office have appeared in the courts during the last ten years on homosexual charges; how many were found guilty; and how many of those found guilty and not guilty respectively are now in Government employment.' The answer soon came. 'I am having the necessary enquiries made. When these have been completed, I shall write to my honourable and gallant Friend.'

Whatever Mr Heath, to the left of Conservative thinking, thought of Captain Kerby, he was bound by parliamentary courtesy to address him as both 'honourable' (all MPs are 'honourable' even if they most patently are not) and 'gallant' (acknowledging Captain Kerby's officer status), and of course, being members of the same party, they are by definition 'friends'. There are no hard and fast rules as to how you can describe a fellow Member of Parliament, but the guidelines have evolved over the years, with rulings by the Speaker defining proper Westminster conduct. A Member cannot call a fellow Member drunk, but can state, as James Wellbeloved, then Labour MP for Erith and Crayford, did in 1974, 'I am not suggesting that they are drunk. I am merely suggesting they are giving a very good imitation of it.'

'Liar' is not permissible, but 'hamster' is all right. When Roderick Richards, Conservative MP for Clwyd North West, called Labour MP Peter Hain a liar during a 1994 debate, he earned a stern and prompt rebuke from Madam Speaker, but it did not prevent him from being promoted to a junior position at the Welsh Office a few days later. Two years earlier a Labour Member had referred to Tories 'telling porkies', and the Speaker had to look the phrase up in a dictionary (presumably one of rhyming slang) after the debate. Once she discovered what it meant, she insisted that 'the Honourable Member should please withdraw it', which he reluctantly did.

Why should it be fine to call a fellow Member 'a pig's bladder on a stick', for example, which has long since been allowed by historical precedent, but not a 'Nosey Parker', which was banned during a debate in 1955? There is no comprehensive list of unparliamentary language, but when a word or phrase is ruled unparliamentary by the Speaker, the MP who used the offending phrase must withdraw it. If he or she does not, they may be 'named', which has the effect of banning them from the chamber for a period. It is apparently OK to repeat within the House the Norwegian word '*dritsek*' which was used by the Norwegian Minister of Agriculture to describe his British counterpart John Selwyn Gummer, even though the English translation of the word would be unacceptable. It reminds me of the Japanese politician who used a strong phrase on one of his political opponents during a debate: the official translation was 'Go to hell – honourably.'

Official translations can cause major diplomatic incidents. Even John F. Kennedy's famous statement at the Berlin Wall, '*Ich bin ein Berliner*', caused difficulties. What he meant was, 'I am a Berliner', and what he should have said was '*Ich bin Berliner.*' The use of the indefinite article '*ein*' meant that he had described himself as a particular type of sticky cake popular in Central Europe, rather than as a citizen of the then beleaguered city. President Carter's interpreter during a visit to Poland managed to transform the President's innocent state-

ment to the effect that America wanted to be friends with the Polish people into a desire to make love to the entire Polish nation. Carter, who had once admitted to *Playboy* magazine that he had lusted after other women, which was 'being unfaithful in his thoughts', had not expected such a libidinous offer ever to be made in his name, and it is not certain how many Poles asked to take him up on his offer. At an EC conference on agricultural matters in the 1980s, the French delegate referred to a particular problem in Normandy requiring local farming knowhow to solve properly. In French, he opined that '*la sagesse des Normands*' would put matters right. The official translation brought howls of laughter from the British and Irish delegates, and almost caused the conference to collapse. The interpreter had said, entirely correctly, that 'to solve this problem, we need Norman Wisdom'. Even when the joke was explained to the French delegates, they did not understand, and no doubt feared a dastardly Anglo-Saxon trick.

At least Norman Wisdom did not cause a fight to break out. In some parliaments fights seem to be commonplace. In Taiwan,

MPs seem to prefer physical to verbal debate, something which also occurs in many other Asian parliaments, but in Britain the nearest anybody has got to hitting anybody else in the Chamber is when Michael Heseltine picked up the mace and waved it about him during a particularly emotional point in a debate. This caused uproar, of course, which is one of the things that the House does not tolerate. Unlike many national parliaments, which are fully wired for sound and where speakers stand on a podium in front of a microphone to address their fellow members, the Palace of Westminster has only recently been dragged, like a reluctant maiden aunt on to the dance floor, into the age of broadcasting. Thus a voice that carries to the farthest recesses of the Chamber has always been prized among members. Even so, on 17 June 1963 the speaker was forced to interrupt questions being put to the then Joint Parliamentary Secretary to the Ministry of Pensions and National Insurance, with the plea, 'I must ask the House to exercise some restraint about the number of decibels in conversation.' The Joint Parliamentary Secretary to the Ministry of Pensions and National Insurance in question was Mrs Margaret Thatcher.

If there is one thing worse than speaking too loud, it is wearing clothes that are too loud. Sir Nicholas Fairbairn, who died in February 1995, was the natural successor to the likes of Norman St John-Stevas and Sir Gerald Nabarro as the dandy of the House, but none of those three dapper dressers ever had a point of order taken against him for trying to vote in his pyjamas, as once happened to Winston Churchill. Voting in pyjamas, while never a necessity (and it would be hard to imagine one of Sir Winston's successors, Margaret Thatcher, voting in her nightie: perhaps only Alan Clark would dare to imagine it), is

made more likely by the bizarre hours that the House of Commons has always followed. By 1995 steps were being taken to rationalize the business hours of the House, so that all-night sessions would become less frequent, and ludicrously long sessions like the one which ran non-stop from 4 p.m. on 31 January 1881 to 9.30 a.m. on 2 February, discussing the question of Better Protection for Person and Property in Ireland, will become things of the past. When the business of the House is so important, even if the discussion does so little good that a century later there is still no satisfactory answer to the problem, it is not surprising that our gallant law-makers put in such long hours at the office. Typical subjects for debate in 1976–7 – to take a session at random – include the Beef Cow Subsidy Payment Order, the Herring (Restrictions on Landing) Order, the Deer (Nightly Close Time) Bill, Fair Play for Children in Scotland, Asbestos in Hair Dryers, Japanese Seaweed in the Solent and the Nutritional Standard of Soup; all are subjects well worth missing a good night's sleep for. And, of course, the Protection of People and Property in Ireland. Twelve years later – another session taken at random – MPs had advanced these matters so far that they were discussing the Self-Governing Schools Etc. (Scotland) Bill, the Water Bill and a White Paper entitled 'Food Safety – Protecting the Consumer', which not only elaborated upon the nutritional standard of all types of soup, but also involved the young daughter of the Minister in charge, Mr John Selwyn Gummer, eating a ropey-looking hamburger for the benefit of press photographers.

Some bills are more trouble than they are worth. On 11 May 1977, the Government admitted it had made a mistake in introducing the Acts of Parliament (Correction of Mistakes) Bill to the House. The Act had been meant to enable the House to correct grammatical and typographical errors in past statutes, which in their present form were rendered unworkable. However, there were too many flaws in the Acts of Parliament (Correction of Mistakes) Bill for MPs to be satisfied it actually would correct the mistakes which everybody admitted did exist in many other Acts. Lady Birk, Under-Secretary of State for the Environment, in discussing the Bill in the Lords, gave one example of the Rent (Agriculture) Bill, which had had 129 amendments inserted into it between 6.15 p.m. and 7.30 p.m. one night in November 1976. The inevitable result of this flurry of activity was that a wrong amendment was inserted in the Bill when the Commons considered the changes made in the Lords, and the resultant Act, which moved successfully on to the statute book, was, in Lady Birk's words, 'a load of nonsense'. There is still no Acts of Parliament (Correction of Mistakes) Bill, even though we quite clearly need one.

Bills vary in length as much as speeches discussing them do.

In general, their importance is in inverse proportion to their length. One of the major items of legislation of the century, the Parliament (Qualification of Women) Act of 1918, is only 28 words long, while the Abdication Bill of December 1936 was not only short but passed all its stages, including Royal Assent, within eight hours. The Merchant Shipping Act of 1894, on the other hand, contains 748 different sections, and Barbara Castle's Transport Bill of the late 1960s was the longest thus far introduced to the Commons. The Maastricht Treaty, which is both significant and impenetrable, is 60,000 words long, the length of a decent thriller. It is not such a snappy read as a decent thriller, although there is at least one recorded case of the Treaty being read at one go. About 500 children took part in a marathon charity reading of the Maastricht Treaty at John Ellis Community College in Leicester on Tuesday 17 November 1992. There are better ways of spending Tuesdays in November, even in Leicester, but it is the first recorded instance of a large group of people agreeing that the Treaty was actually doing some good.

The British Prime Minister has to pay much more attention to his Parliament, and spend much more time within its walls, than most other Prime Ministers around the world. As John Major said after the EU Summit at Essen in 1994, 'Prime Ministers elsewhere don't find themselves subject to the same rigorous questioning in their parliaments as we do.' Passing over the question of whether he was using the royal 'we' in the manner of his predecessor ('We are a grandmother'), Mr Major has a point. 'Some of my fellow heads of government could scarcely find their way to their parliaments with a guide dog.' The Spanish, Portuguese and Greek Prime Ministers in particular have never been used to detailed cross-examination from within their own parliament buildings, although in Sweden, Members of Parliament and, indeed, voters have the right to inspect the Prime Minister's correspondence. In Britain, we could never go that far. The 30-year rule, which keeps Cabinet papers (and anything else decreed by the government of the day to be sensitive or secret) out of the public arena for 30 years, effectively means that there is little opportunity for political point-scoring by looking at letters exchanged at least six parliaments ago.

The political will of any parliament is put into action by the ministries of the government. The rule of thumb when looking at the structure of any government is that ministries are created to do a job that is either not being done at all, or else is being done unnecessarily but too well. Orwell knew that War is Peace, Freedom is Slavery and Ignorance is Strength, so that when, for example, Pakistan creates a Ministry of Narcotics Control, this implies that it does everything except actually control narcotics. If Trinidad and Tobago has a Ministry of Works, Infrastructure and Decentralization, that is because there is no Infrastructure and no likelihood or political desire for Decentralization. Britain has only appointed Ministers for Industrial Relations when strikes are all around, and Ministers for Sport when we haven't won an international game of anything more taxing than tiddlywinks for several decades. George Brown was appointed to head up a new Department of Economic Affairs at a time when Britain's economy was being run almost exclusively by the International Monetary Fund, and everybody was, as always, trying to keep any other kind of Affairs out of the public eye. We appoint a Minister for Open Government at precisely the same time that other Cabinet Ministers happily justify intense secrecy as being in the public interest. Haiti has a Minister of Planning and External Co-operation, which are two things notable by their absence in that unfortunate country. Greece even has a Ministry of Culture.

Some countries have ministries with names of startling frankness, implying that democracy is low on their list of priorities. The People's Republic of China has a Ministry of Supervision, Mauritania a Ministry of State Control, and the Czech Republic a Ministry of Inspection. South Korea has a National Security Planning Agency, and India has a Ministry of Public Grievances. One of the most optimistic titles for a Ministry is Mongolia's State Control Committee for Nature and the Environment. Earthquakes, floods and famines can apparently be eliminated with the stroke of a ministerial pen. Romania has a Minister of State for the Quality of Life and Social Protection, one of the more sinister ministries of the world. The Soviet Union, on the other hand, gave all its

ministries remarkably bland names, and remarkably long-serving ministers. Pyotr Lomako was the Soviet Minister of Non-Ferrous Metallurgy for 46 years, from 1940 to 1 November 1986, while Andrei Gromyko was Foreign Minister for 28 years until being elected President on 2 July 1985. Everywhere seems to have a Ministry of Justice, often combined with Prisons, although the old South African government included a Ministry of Justice, a Ministry of Law and Order and a Ministry of Correctional Services and Budget. That was because there was not much justice, little law and order, but rather too many correctional services. A recent Mauritanian Minister of Justice gloried in the name of Sow Samba Sow, proving that in that part of Africa at least, if the police were not pigs, their ultimate boss might well have been.

Modernity is creeping up on the political process all around the world. In Britain we still have traditions which govern the rules on how to dress, speak and behave in Parliament. There are also recondite traditions governing such obscure items as the Cap of Maintenance, which was sent to Henry VIII by the Pope, who did not explain at the time exactly what it was used for. Ever since, it has been carried on a custom-made baton in front of the sovereign at the State Opening of Parliament. We have Black Rod, who knocks at the doors of the House of Commons (which have been symbolically barred to him) to summon members to the Upper Chamber to hear the Queen's Speech, and we have the cry of 'Hats off Strangers' from the duty sergeant as the Speaker processes through the lobbies at the start of each parliamentary day. British democracy would not collapse without these traditions, but life for our elected representatives would be less colourful, if also less confusing, without them. The Russians, who are leaping headlong into the twenty-first century having spent the entire twentieth century enmeshed in nineteenth-century Marxist philosophy, have not only shelled their own parliament building in an attempt to persuade political opponents of the force of their arguments, but have also supplied every one of the 450 members of the Duma with laptop computers to make their lives easier. At least 250 have no idea how to turn them on, let alone program them. Perhaps the Russians should have their own version of *Hansard*, the official record of the transactions of the British Parliament, to keep them up to date. It is certainly less stress-inducing than laptop computer technology. At Charles Dickens's home at Gad's Hill, the great author had book spines painted on to a fake bookcase: 19 of the spines read 'Hansard's Guide to Refreshing Sleep'.

SUPPLEMENTARIES

Curious Ministries:

Ministry of Handlooms and Textiles Industries; Sri Lanka

Ministry of Housing Co-operatives; Belize

Ministry of Pilgrimage and Endowments; Saudi Arabia

Ministry of Public Grievances; India

Ministry of State (Grains and Oilseeds); Canada

Ministry of State for Administrative Reform; Indonesia

Ministry of Youth, Equality and Ecclesiastical Affairs; Sweden

Members of Parliament accorded an official Vote of Thanks:

Sir Edward Seymour, 17 March 1700

Sir Winston Churchill, 28 July 1964

Black politicians in white governments:

Lord Constantine of Maraval and Nelson, first black West Indian to take seat in House of Lords, 1969

Charles Curtis, Vice-President to Herbert Hoover 1929 to 1933, was one quarter Kansa Indian

Sir S. P. Sinha, first Indian to become a member of a British government, 1919. Also first Indian in House of Lords

Robert Weaver, first black Cabinet member in USA, Secretary of Housing and Urban Development, 1965

Foreign Secretaries who have become Prime Minister:

Earl of Rosebery, J. Ramsay MacDonald, Sir Anthony Eden, Harold Macmillan, Sir Alec Douglas-Home, James Callaghan, John Major

Chancellors of the Exchequer who have become Prime Minister:

Benjamin Disraeli, William Gladstone, Herbert Asquith, David Lloyd George, Andrew Bonar Law, Stanley Baldwin, Winston Churchill, Neville Chamberlain, Harold Macmillan, James Callaghan, John Major

Home Secretaries who have become Prime Minister:

Herbert Asquith, James Callaghan

James Callaghan is the only man to have held all three major offices of State before becoming Prime Minister.

MEN AND WOMEN OF THE PEOPLE

When the British skiffle singer Lonnie Donegan had a heart bypass operation in the 1980s, the Tokyo stock exchange Nikkei Index suffered a massive if brief fall in value. This seems a surprising reaction to the condition of a mere musician, even one who had three No. 1 hits in the ten years before the Beatles changed the pop music industry, but the reason was not hard to find. A Japanese broker, reading the wires from the States, mistook the name of Lonnie Donegan for that of Ronnie Reagan, then President of the United States.

The incident highlighted a strange political anomaly, first noticed by Alistair Cooke: music and politics do not mix. Cooke pointed out that, in their memoirs, none of the pre-war generation of British politicians such as Bonar Law, Asquith, Lloyd George or Balfour expressed the slightest interest in music, and the 1st Lord Birkenhead (F. E. Smith, Lloyd George's Lord Chancellor) was so tone deaf that he had to be nudged into a standing position every time the National Anthem was played. One of Lonnie Donegan's two American top ten hits was 'Does Your Chewing Gum Lose Its Flavour?', which included lines about being sent 'up to the White House, the nation's only White House, to voice our discontent unto the President, upon the burning question that has swept the continent', namely whether your chewing gum does indeed lose its flavour on the bedpost overnight. Despite this obvious link between music and politics, history has shown that musical and political talent are mutually exclusive – or very nearly so. There is Sir Edward Heath, British Prime Minister from 1970 to 1974, who was an organ scholar at Balliol College, Oxford, and who was reported to have attended a Rod Stewart concert at Olympia at Christmas 1976. This highly unlikely happening is mentioned in the 1994 biography of Stewart by Ray Coleman, who believes that Heath, 'a keen yachtsman, was probably attracted to Rod because of his hit "Sailing"'. That story seems to be a curiosity that should be taken with a pinch of salt water.

Other genuinely musical politicians include Ignace Paderewski (1860–1941), the concert pianist who became the first Prime Minister of the reconstituted Poland after the First World War, and subsequently its President. Billy Hughes, then Prime Minister of Australia, told Paderewski at the Versailles Peace Conference to 'take his policy home and play it on the piano', so we can safely assume that Hughes himself was another politician with no great love of music. We should mention Jan Masaryk, the Czech Foreign Minister immediately after the Second World War, whose only pleasure, according to David Low the political cartoonist, was to play the piano, but then the list seems to stop. Masaryk's fatal defenestration in 1947 was seen as a comment on his politics rather than his piano playing.

The rock generation of politicians is represented by President Clinton, who plays the saxophone without any real distinction, and Tony Blair, who was educated at Durham Choristers'

School and was once a member of an unsigned and probably untalented band called Ugly Rumours. Clinton's awareness of music may be aptly summed up by his use of Fleetwood Mac's 'Don't Stop' as his election theme tune: the song was from their multi-million selling *Rumours* album, which dealt musically with infidelities and the break-up of relationships within the band, something which President Clinton, who never inhaled, knows nothing about, of course. Athol Guy, once a member of the chart-topping but hardly rocking group the Seekers, subsequently became an Australian State Senator, and Sonny Bono, half of the chart-topping folk rock duo Sonny and Cher, became a Republican Congressman in 1994. Mike Curb, producer of the teenybopping Osmonds, became Lieutenant-Governor of California, which surely proves that only people with no feel for music can become successful politicians. Miss Betty Boothroyd, once a high-stepping member of the Tiller Girls dance troupe, became a Labour MP in 1974 and subsequently Speaker of the House of Commons in 1992. Screaming Lord Sutch, a hitless 1960s rock and roller, holds the British record for most elections fought (over 30) and most deposits lost (over 30), making him uniquely unsuccessful in both spheres.

Margaret Thatcher is one of the few politicians to have had a hit song written about her while she was still in power – a track called 'Stand Down Margaret' by the Beat reached No. 22 in the British charts in 1980 – but her knowledge of music is such that she probably never knew of this doubtful honour. Her favourite songs were widely reported to have been 'How Much Is That Doggie in the Window?' (a paean to free enterprise and care in the community) and 'Telstar', by the Tornadoes, a British tune inspired by American technology. She also took advantage of an opportunity in 1987 to be photographed in the Abbey Road studios sitting in front of a drum kit, which she appeared to be about to browbeat. Her one attempt at making a hit record, a melodramatic version of Lincoln's Gettysburg Address, failed to win her many new fans.

When Keir Hardie was first elected as a Labour MP in 1892, he processed to the Palace of Westminster, preceded by a cornetist playing the 'Marseillaise', no doubt considered a suitably revolutionary tune for the first working-class member of Britain's ruling body.

Musicians have always tried to take an interest in politics, despite the clear lack of interest in their efforts by the politicians, and their staggeringly naïve outlook on most political issues. The late Leonard Bernstein shocked the 1960s American political establishment and established his radical chic qualifications by throwing a party for the urban guerrilla Black Panther Movement. Since the days of Woody Guthrie and Bob

Dylan, the protest song has been an alternative political art form in America. In more recent years, Paul Weller and Billy Bragg, British chart-toppers both, combined to create Red Wedge, a politically aware group whose music during the 1987 election campaign proved once again that politics cannot easily be put to music, and it doesn't help the political cause even if it is. The Conservatives made use of the talents of Vince Hill during the 1979 and 1983 elections, in 1979 to record 'Hello Maggie' to the tune of 'Hello Dolly', and in 1983 to rework 'Hundreds of Girls' from the flop musical *Mack and Mabel* as 'It's Maggie for Me'. By 1987 Mr Hill had decided against further ventures into the murky waters of political musicality. So the Tories turned to Sir Andrew Lloyd Webber to compose a tune for the 1987 election: bearing in mind the fact that the only political woman Sir Andrew had previously dealt with in music was Eva Perón, a whore and a swindler on a majestic scale, it was brave of Mrs Thatcher to commission him. *Evita*, the Tim Rice/Andrew Lloyd Webber musical based on the life of the wife of the Argentine President Juan Perón, is undoubtedly the most successful collaboration of politics and music in recent times. The hit song 'Don't Cry For Me Argentina' has passed into popular cliché.

There have been other political musicals, notably *Pins and Needles*, which opened on Broadway in November 1937 and ran for 1,108 performances, then a record. The musical was originally presented by the International Ladies Garment Workers Union and included such numbers as 'Sing a Song of Social Significance' and 'Not Cricket to Picket'. The hit dance number was 'Doin' the Reactionary'. Music and lyrics were by Harold Rome, whose next musical, *Sing Out the News*, included the hit song 'FDR Jones'. FDR was also a target in the 1938 musical *Knickerbocker Holiday*, which included one of the great songs of the century, 'September Song'. The play dealt with the life of the seventeenth-century Governor of New York, Peter Stuyvesant, but it was interpreted as an attack on Roosevelt and his cabinet, and ran for only 168 performances.

President François Mitterrand of France is famous for his lack of interest in music, which is taken as a contributory factor in the Opéra Bastille fiasco, a government plan for a second opera house in Paris which was never needed, was barely thought out and finally collapsed in tatters. President Richard Nixon hosted a party at the White House on 29 April 1969 to celebrate the 70th birthday of the distinguished jazzman Duke Ellington. He did himself no favours among the jazz-loving members of the electorate, however, when he warmly greeted another famous guest, Cab Calloway, with the words, 'Ah, Mr Ellington. Happy Birthday.' It was a story that Calloway never tired of retelling.

President McKinley and music were a fatal combination. He was gunned down by Leon Czolgosz in the Temple of

Music at the Pan-American Exposition in September 1901. President Wilson appeared in 1918 at the Metropolitan Opera House, and what is more, his appearance was as a performer rather than as a member of the audience. His performance was, however, strictly non-musical. He made a speech at a rally to drum up popular support for the League of Nations and America's participation in it. One politician who did perform musically at a rally was James Callaghan, then Prime Minister, to the TUC Congress in 1978. He sang a couple of lines of the music hall song, 'There was I, waiting at the church', in what was meant to be a coded reference to his intention not to hold a general election until the following year. However, the TUC misinterpreted his song, and assumed it meant he was going to call a general election very shortly. The political message always tends to get lost in music.

However, it would be wrong to suggest that, just because politicians as a breed are not musicians, they do not share other interests of the populations they represent. The American political commentator Clinton Rossiter pointed out that a president does not have to be an intellectual giant, but he does have to like 'baseball, detective stories, fishing, pop concerts, picnics, dogs and seascapes'. Well, forget the pop concerts, maybe, but it would be political suicide for a politician not to be an animal lover. Ever since the Roman Emperor Caligula appointed his horse Incitatus a consul, animals have had an important role to play in politics. Jimmie Davis, country singer and Governor of Louisiana, once rode his favourite cow pony up the steps of the Capitol, thus combining politics, music and animals in one grand but entirely useless gesture. Sir Robert Peel, English Prime Minister in the 1830s and 1840s, and

Captain Terence O'Neill, Prime Minister of Northern Ireland in the 1960s, both died after falls from a horse, but the 5th Earl of Rosebery was more lucky. He had three ambitions: to marry an heiress, to become Prime Minister and to own a Derby winner. He managed all three: firstly, by marrying Hannah, daughter of Baron Meyer de Rothschild; secondly, by becoming Liberal Prime Minister of the United Kingdom on Gladstone's retirement in 1894; and thirdly, by owning Ladas, which won the Derby in 1894, Sir Visto, which won the following year, and Cicero, which won after he had left Number Ten, in 1905.

When the late Sir James Scott-Hopkins was elected as Conservative Member for North Cornwall in 1959, it coincided with the youngest daughter of the Revd Templeman Speer, Rector of Lanteglos by Camelford, going to boarding school. She therefore had to find a new home for her bantam hens, which could not accompany her to the wilds of Devon. The new MP was approached, and he gladly took them home for his own four children (and for the eggs). Such was his dedication to his new profession as a politician that he named all the chickens after members of the Cabinet, from Harold Macmillan downwards. It did not cause his children to imagine all politicians were scrawny-necked skinny-legged chickens, either, for 21 years later his daughter Jennifer kept her place in the political pecking order by marrying Tim Smith, now Conservative MP for Beaconsfield. Whether they keep bantams is unrecorded.

Dogs have played their part in national politics as well. President Lyndon Johnson got into trouble for picking his pet beagles up by their ears in front of the Press corps, but as he treated most of his Cabinet officers far worse than that, it did not seem to upset the electorate too much. When the Governor-General of Australia, the 3rd Lord Denman, laid the foundation stone of the new federal capital city, Canberra, on 12 March 1913, all of the new nation's pomp and circumstance was there. As His Excellency stepped back to admire his handiwork, a small brown mongrel dog wandered out from the crowd, cocked his leg and christened the stone. Australia has always been the home of the vulgar gesture. Offa, the guide dog of David Blunkett, the blind Labour MP, had a less ceremonial role but was the first dog to take a seat in the House of Commons in 1987. Offa's successor, Lucy, was the second. Harold Wilson was reportedly saved from drowning by his family Labrador, Paddy, while Matthew Parris, Conservative MP for West Derbyshire from 1979 to 1986, won an RSPCA bravery award for saving a dog from drowning.

Winston Churchill loved dogs and often praised people for showing 'the canine virtues' of loyalty to friends, 'particularly in foul weather'. This view of virtue did not stop Churchill from crossing the floor of the House twice in his parliamentary career, a curious history of not being loyal to friends for somebody who went on to lead his nation. Lloyd George famously described the House of Lords as 'Mr Balfour's poodle', while Lord Robert Cecil called the Treasury Ministers 'monkeys at the zoo' in June 1914.

Perhaps the most famous political dog, at least in the United States, was Checkers, a dog whose existence was to have a profound effect on Western politics in the latter part of the twentieth century. Checkers was a spaniel which in 1952 belonged to Tricia and Julie, the two young daughters of the then Senator Richard Nixon, who was Dwight D. Eisenhower's running mate in that year's presidential election. Nixon was accused of using campaign donations for his own private purposes, a charge which he denied in an emotional television broadcast to the nation. The only campaign gift which he said he had accepted and had every intention of keeping was the cuddly Checkers. His obvious sincerity turned the tide of public opinion back in his favour, and he stayed on the ticket to become Vice-President for eight years. If Checkers had been a rottweiler rather than a spaniel, the course of history might have been changed. Curiously, Eisenhower himself was not a dog man: he much preferred cats.

President Nixon, as he later became, was a participant in the panda diplomacy which the Chinese conducted with foreign leaders as they tried to reintroduce themselves into the international family of nations in the 1970s. British Prime Minister Edward Heath was the first to receive a panda, which he donated to London Zoo, but within a decade it seemed that most world leaders had their own private panda chew-

ing bamboo shoots behind bars in their nation's leading zoo. Gandhi preferred less exotic animals. When he came to Britain for the India Round Table Conference of 1931, he arrived with an entourage consisting of his 'disciple' Madeleine Slade, and two goats. The goats' opinion of the India question or the proceedings of the conference is not recorded.

Many politicians have been fine sportsmen, despite the late Lord Campbell of Eskan's comment that 'people can't understand how I can be a Socialist and also good at games'. At the end of 1994, the Brazilian government appointed Edson Arantes do Nascimento, otherwise known as Pele, the most famous footballer of all time, as Minister of Sport. At the same time there were two Olympic athletes who were British MPs – Sebastian Coe, Conservative MP for Truro, Olympic gold medallist at 1,500 metres in both 1980 and 1984 and still holder of the world 800 metres record, and Menzies Campbell, Liberal Democrat MP for Fife North East, who competed in the 1964 Olympics in Tokyo, and was British record holder for the 100 metres from 1965 to 1974. Jeffrey Archer, MP for Louth from 1969 to 1974 before the first of several minor career setbacks caused him to resign, represented Great Britain as a sprinter in 1966, without, however, ever quite reaching Olympic standard.

Harold Wilson's first Minister for Sport, the Rt Hon. Denis Howell, appointed in 1969, was a Football League referee from 1956 to 1970, though his main claim to fame stems from his brief period from 1974 as Minister with Responsibility for Water Resources, otherwise popularly known as the Minister for Drought. Within days of his appointment, the months-long drought which he was supposed to deal with had broken with a series of spectacular downpours and his success in the job was assured. Harold Wilson was never a great sportsman himself, but he took great pride in the fact that he was Prime Minister on the only occasion that England ever won the World Cup, an event which was to influence his decision-making four years later. By 1970 a general election was becoming due, and Wilson worried over the timing. If he were to call the election in June, England would be defending their World Cup title in Mexico at the same time. Defeat for the English team might dent the Government's re-election chances. However, when he learnt that the matches would only be on television very late at night, he decided to ignore the World Cup factor. Perhaps he should not have done. England were beaten 3–2 by West Germany in the quarter-finals on 14 June 1970, and four days later Labour were defeated at the polls. One can only assume that Wilson knew that much of his party's most fervent support was in Scotland and Wales, where an England defeat would have been welcomed as a fine government initiative. One of his senior lieutenants, Denis Healey, clearly had no idea of the significance of the event, and he remains one of Parliament's least sporting members. In his memoirs, he writes of 'the British football team' defending the World Cup in Argentina. Wrong team, wrong location – the story of too many election campaigns.

Lord Dalmeny, later the 6th Earl of Rosebery, was a Middlesex cricketer before he became Liberal MP for Midlothian in 1910, and Ted Dexter, England Test cricketer and much later Chairman of the Selectors, stood unsuccessfully as a Conservative candidate against James Callaghan in Cardiff South East in 1964. John Arlott, the poet and cricket broadcaster, stood unsuc-

cessfully as Liberal candidate for Epping in both the 1955 and 1959 elections. The most famous cricketing parliamentarian, however, is Lord Home, who as Sir Alec Douglas-Home was Prime Minister from 1963 to 1964, and as Lord Dunglass played in ten first-class matches between 1924 and 1927. Christopher Chataway, the middle-distance runner and BBC Sports Personality of 1954, was Conservative MP for Lewisham North from 1959 to 1966 and for Chichester from 1969 to 1974, during which time he rose to the rank of Minister of Posts and Telecommunications and subsequently Minister for Industrial Development. It is not clear whether breaking the 5,000 metres world record in 1954 was a good preparation for his political career, but when he said he was going to run for Parliament, everybody knew he would be hard to beat. The only British politician since Lord Rosebery to reach the sporting heights after his election to the House of Commons is, however, Edward Heath, who skippered his yacht *Morning Cloud* to victory in the Sydney to Hobart Ocean Race in 1969, when he was already Leader of the Opposition. He was Captain of Britain's Admiral's Cup team in 1971, when he was Prime Minister.

In America, basketball Hall of Fame member and 1964 Olympic gold medallist Bill Bradley has been a Senator for New Jersey since 1979, and Gerald Ford, US President from 1974 to 1977, was offered professional football terms by both the Chicago Bears and the Detroit Lions. Fred Perry, Wimbledon men's singles champion for three years from 1934 to 1936 and Britain's most successful male tennis player of all time, was the son of Samuel Perry, Labour MP for Kettering, who was a minister in Ramsay MacDonald's Labour administration from 1929 to 1931. Perry senior was one of several Labour ministers who refused to serve in the National Government from 1931, which he viewed as a sell-out of Socialist principles. Although all the ministerial rebels were offered peerages as an appeasement, Perry turned his down. If he had not, Britain's most recent Wimbledon men's champion would have been a member of the aristocracy.

Lavrenti Beria, Stalin's dreaded chief of the NKVD secret police, was a keen football supporter, having played for Dynamo Tbilisi in his youth. He naturally had a particular interest in the fortunes of the NKVD team, Moscow Dynamo. Beria organized the arrest in 1936 of the president of their arch rivals, Moscow Spartak, and of the three Starostin brothers, who were Spartak's star players. All four spent years in prison camps, but even with this advantage Dynamo did not entirely overshadow their rivals. Dynamo won the championship in 1936, 1937, 1940, 1945 and 1949, and the cup in 1937 and in 1953, the year Beria was executed, but Spartak won both championship and cup five times each in the same period.

Kim Jong Il, leader of North Korea since the death of his father in 1994, and a man as strongly democratic as Beria, was playing at Pyongyang Golf Club in 1994 when he shot five holes in one and completed the 18 holes in 34 strokes, according to the club professional, who knows how to keep his job secure. That is 25 shots better than the previous world record, 59, by the American professional Al Geiberger. Kim Jong Il's record has not been officially ratified, but if he is ever overthrown, he clearly will represent as much of a threat to the livelihoods of Nick Faldo and Greg Norman as he currently does to the entire North Korean people.

Robin Squire, Conservative MP for Hornchurch since 1979, showed his lack of sensitivity towards sport when he defeated the former Tottenham and England footballer Jimmy Greaves in the selection process for his seat. However, his election in 1979, and his re-election three times since then, owes nothing, we are assured, to his skills as a hypnotist. Although he is a former President of the Federation of Stage Hypnotists (the subject of parliamentary debate at the end of 1994), he has never asked the electorate to look him closely in the eye and obey his every command, including putting a cross against his

name in the polling booth. It must be that his political instincts overcome his hypnotic ones, as no politician ever wants to look anybody in the eye.

SUPPLEMENTARIES

MP with platinum, gold and silver discs as a gospel singer:

Revd William McCrea (DUP, Ulster Mid)

MPs who have appeared in pop videos include:

Neil Kinnock (in 'My Guy' by Tracey Ullman), Merlyn Rees, Sir Cyril Smith

Hit records about real politicians include:

'Abraham, Martin and John' by Dion, No. 4 in US, 1968

'Abraham, Martin and John' by Marvin Gaye, No. 9 in Britain, 1970

'Biko' by Peter Gabriel, No. 38 in Britain, 1980

'Nelson Mandela' by the Specials, No. 9 in Britain, 1984

'Sha La La' by Manfred Mann, No. 3 in Britain, 1964, is *not* about Donna Shalala, President Clinton's Secretary of Health and Human Resources.

Flop records about real politicians include:

'Bridge over Troubled Water' by Harold and Ted, coupled with '7½% Swing' by the Floating Voters, Pye 7N 17960, issued 1970

'The President Song' by Victor Trumper, MCA 40260, issued 1974

Politicians who have had hit records include:

Senator Everett Dirksen, 'Gallant Men', No. 29 in US, 1967

Malcolm X, 'No Sell Out', No. 60 in Britain, 1984

Sir Winston Churchill, 'The Voice of Sir Winston Churchill' LP, No. 6 in Britain, 1965

President John F. Kennedy, seven tribute albums in the two years after his death, including 'A Memorial Album', which sold over 500,000 copies early in 1964

Nana Mouskouri, Greek MEP since 1994, has been recording for over 35 years, with three top ten hit albums in Britain, and one No. 2 hit single, 'Only Love'.

Politicians who have written songs:

Rep. Salvatore 'Sonny' Bono, elected to Congress in 1994, co-wrote 'Needles and Pins', a No. 1 hit for the Searchers in 1964, and 'I Got You Babe', a No. 1 hit for Sonny and Cher in 1965 and for UB40 with Chrissie Hynde in 1985.

Jimmie Davis, Governor of Louisiana from 1944 to 1948 and from 1960 to 1964, was elected to the Country Music Hall of Fame in 1972. He wrote 'You Are My Sunshine' and 'Nobody's Darling but Mine' among many others.

Charles Gates Dawes, Vice-President to Calvin Coolidge, wrote the tune of 'It's All in the Game', a No. 1 hit in both Britain and America for Tommy Edwards.

Derek Enright, Labour MP for Hemsworth since 1991, has written Latin lyrics for two Beatles' songs, and ancient Greek lyrics for another, 'Yesterday'.

Politicians who have appeared in films include:

Rep. Bella Abzug played herself in Woody Allen's *Manhattan* (1979).

Nancy, Lady Astor, first British woman to take her seat in the House of Commons, appeared in *Royal Cavalcade* (1935).

Lord Boothby, Conservative peer and former MP, and Michael Foot, Labour MP for Ebbw Vale, both appeared in *Rockets Galore* (1958).

Horatio Bottomley, Liberal MP for South Hackney from 1906 to 1912 and 1918 to 1922, appeared in *Was It He?* (1914).

Chief Mangosuthu Buthelezi, South African Inkatha Freedom Party leader, played his own great-great-great-great grandfather in *Zulu* (1964).

Sebastian Coe, Conservative MP for Falmouth, played himself in an episode of the BBC TV situation comedy, *The Brittas Empire* (1993).

Josephus Daniels, US Secretary of the Navy from 1913, played himself in *Victory* (1913).

Moshe Dayan, Israeli Minister of Defence, and Yitzhak Rabin, Israel's Prime Minister, both played themselves in *Operation Thunderbolt* (1977).

Georgi Dmitrov, Prime Minister of Bulgaria from 1946 to 1949, appeared in *Kämpfer* (1936).

Andrew Faulds, Labour MP for Warley East, appeared in over 35 films, and also played the part of Jet Morgan in the BBC's *Journey Into Space*.

John Gorton, Prime Minister of Australia from 1968 to 1971, appeared in *Don's Party* (1976).

Vice-President Hubert Humphrey and Senator George McGovern, Democratic presidential nominee in 1972, both played themselves in *The Candidate* (1972).

Glenda Jackson, Labour MP for Hampstead since 1992, won two Oscars as Best Actress – in 1971 for her role in *Women in Love* and in 1974 for her role in *A Touch of Class*. Her *Who's Who* entry lists over 30 films.

Jomo Kenyatta, first President of Kenya, played the role of a minor African chief in *Sanders of the River* (1934).

Mao Zedong, Chairman of the Chinese Communist Party, starred in *Chairman Mao Reviews the Mighty Contingent of the Cultural Revolution for the Fifth and Sixth Times* (1967).

Mrs Pat Nixon, wife of President Richard Nixon, appeared in *Becky Sharp* (1936) and *Small Town Girl* (1937).

Ignace Paderewski, Prime Minister of Poland, appeared in *Moonlight Sonata* (1937).

Ronald Reagan, US President from 1981 to 1989, starred in many films, including *Love Is on the Air* (1937), *Tugboat Annie Sails Again* (1940), *Knute Rockne, All American* (1940), *Bedtime for Bonzo* (1951) and *The Killers* (1964).

Presidents Theodore Roosevelt and Woodrow Wilson appeared as themselves in the 1917 film, *Womanhood: The Glory of a Nation.*

Leon Trotsky, Russian revolutionary, played the role of a nihilist in the US production, *My Official Wife* (1914).

Gough Whitlam, Prime Minister of Australia from 1972 to 1975, appeared as himself in *Barry McKenzie Holds His Own* (1974).

Politicians who have written novels:

Winston Churchill, *Savrola*

Edwina Currie MP, *A Parliamentary Affair*

Benjamin Disraeli, *Vivian Grey, Coningsby, Sybil, Tancred*

Wilfred Fienburgh, Labour MP from 1951 to 1958, *No Love for Johnnie* (1951)

Valéry Giscard d'Estaing, former President of France, *Le Passage*

Roy Hattersley MP, deputy leader of the Labour Party from 1983 to 1992, *The Maker's Mark* (1990), *In That Quiet Earth* (1991)

Benito Mussolini, Il Duce of Italy, *Claudia Particella, or The Cardinal's Love* (1909)

Writers who tried to become politicians include:

Rupert Allason, Conservative MP, has written (as Nigel West) many books on espionage, including *A Matter of Trust: MI5 1945–1972.*

Jeffrey Archer, now Lord Archer, author of *Shall We Tell the President?* and *First Among Equals* among others, was Conservative MP for Louth from 1969 to 1974.

Gyles Brandreth, author of such works as *I Scream for Ice Cream, Yarooh!, Brandreth's Bedroom* and *Even Greater Sexual Disasters*, was elected Conservative MP for Chester in 1992.

Vaclav Havel, playwright, was elected President of Czechoslovakia (later the Czech Republic) in 1989.

Victor Hugo, poet, dramatist and novelist, author of *The Hunchback of Notre Dame*, was elected to the French National Assembly in 1871.

Douglas Hurd, author of *Vote to Kill, The Truth Game* and other thrillers, became a Conservative MP in 1974 and Foreign Secretary in 1989.

Gore Vidal, author of *Myra Breckinridge* and the play *An Evening with Richard Nixon*, stood as Democratic-Liberal candidate for Congress in 1960, and as a candidate for Democratic nomination for election to the US Senate from California in 1982, but failed to be elected.

H. G. Wells was a Labour candidate in the 1922 and 1923 general elections, but was not elected.

Jobs held by politicians before they held political office include:

Robert Adley, Conservative MP: Sales Director for the Mayfair Hotel, London

David Blunkett, Labour MP: East Midlands Gas Board

Robert Clay, Labour MP: bus driver

Sir Anthony Eden, British Prime Minister: arts critic for the *Yorkshire Post*

Rajiv Gandhi, Indian Prime Minister: airline pilot

Andrew Hargreaves, Conservative MP: auctioneer

Ho Chi Minh, leader of North Vietnam: waiter in the bar of the Carlton Hotel, Haymarket, London

Ken Livingstone, Labour MP: cancer research worker

John Major, British Prime Minister: executive in Standard Chartered Bank

John Prescott, British Labour Party deputy leader: merchant seaman

Andrew Rowe, Conservative MP: Eton College assistant master

Henry Wilson, US Vice-President: cobbler

6 MONEY, SEX AND SLEAZE

If there is one truth which we hold to be self-evident about the practice of politics, it is that without money to oil the smooth turning of its wheels, the whole thing would grind very rapidly to a halt. Since the very earliest days, people have tried to buy and sell politicians just as surely as they have tried to buy and sell horses, sex and soap powder. And they are still trying.

Will Rogers, the American film star and politician, may have been right 60 years ago when he said, 'Over there [Britain] politics is an obligation; over here it's a business,' but these days the American attitude has spread eastwards across the

Atlantic. A survey carried out in 1994 showed that 64 per cent of British people believed that 'most MPs make money by abusing their position in Parliament' – an enormous increase from 46 per cent a decade earlier. Professor Ivor Crewe, the politics guru at Essex University, was quoted as believing that 'the British public have taken it for granted that most MPs are self-serving impostors and hypocrites who put party before country and self before party.' But it was always thus, and not just in Britain. Not only is politics power: 'Power tends to corrupt. Absolute power corrupts absolutely.' The man who wrote that, John Emerich Edward Dalberg, 1st Lord Acton, was born in Naples of a British father and a German mother, was educated in Paris and Munich, and spent much of his early adult life in America. He attended the coronation of Tsar Alexander II in 1856 and was Liberal MP for Carlow from 1859 to 1865, so he had plenty of experience of men of power in all the Western civilizations of his time. In his next sentence he stated: 'Great men are almost always bad men.' So it is no curiosity to point out the evils of political men (and women). It goes with the territory. Whether Lord Acton considered himself a great man, and therefore knew himself to be bad, is not known. Perhaps he knew that his only failing was that he was not bad enough to be great.

Even a century ago the leading politicians were looking for ways to make money, or perhaps, to be more accurate, others were finding ways of making money out of leading politicians. In 1877 a somewhat unlikely advertisement appeared in the local Philadelphia newspapers. It showed President and Mrs Hayes sitting in their rooms at the Continental Hotel, with Mrs Hayes holding an iron and saying to her husband, 'We cannot leave until we visit the Enterprise Manufacturing Co. and order some of Mrs Potts' Cold Handle Sad Irons, like this.' To this unlikely piece of loving small talk, Mr President replies, 'But my dear, they are for sale by all hardware stores in this country.' What fee was paid to the Hayeses by Mrs Potts and the Enterprise Manufacturing Company for this remarkable testimonial is not disclosed, but it is good to learn that affairs of state in 1877 were not so pressing that there was not time to visit the local hardware store from time to time. In the 1880 election 'Vote As We Fought' torches supporting the Garfield/Arthur ticket were on sale at 25 cents each. Oil portraits of the candidates, 36 by 48 inches, sold for $10 each, and the larger 48 by 72-inch version at $15. Banners for street processions were a bargain at $20.

We cannot be certain whether Mrs Rutherford Hayes actually used Mrs Potts's Cold Handle Sad Iron, but we can be sure that the publishers of a contemporary print showing Abraham Lincoln 'returning on horseback to his home in Springfield Illinois' after his successful campaign for the presidency in October 1860 were being economical with the truth. Lincoln did not move out of Springfield throughout the entire campaign, so could not have been seen returning on horseback. His only concession to the needs of his party was a brief statement at a local Republican rally in August. Eight years later, General Ulysses S. Grant hid himself away in his Illinois hometown, Galena, to avoid the rough and tumble of the election process, and his successor Rutherford Hayes never left Columbus Ohio during the pre-election months, except once to visit the Centennial Exposition in Philadelphia on 28 October, Ohio Day, less than two weeks before the election.

However, he did make the most of his day trip to Pennsylvania, making half a dozen speeches and shaking hands with about 4,000 people. Four years later, Garfield made no pretence of staying at home. He undertook a full national election tour, during which he spoke at least 70 times. From then on, electioneering became an business.

There is no clear line which distinguishes the business of politics, entirely legal and necessary, from taking financial advantage of politics, which is less admirable. The media seem to know when politics becomes scandal, but to the politicians themselves the distinctions are less obvious. This is perhaps surprising when you consider that many of the biggest crooks who have strayed on to the political playing fields have close links with the media who are so eager to blow the whistle and issue red cards. Robert Maxwell, MP for Buckingham during his only slightly crooked days, when the most heinous crime of which he was accused was that of stealing from the House of Commons wine cellars, went on to become a major newspaper owner, in the tradition established half a century earlier by Horatio Bottomley, who, apart from being a swindler on the grand scale, also owned the *Sun*, and founded both *John Bull* magazine and the *Financial Times*. An admiring entry in an encyclopaedia published in 1920 states that Bottomley, Liberal MP for Hackney from 1906 to 1912 and again from 1918, 'became mainly known for the skill with which he conducted his own case in various lawsuits'. When that particular skill deserted him and he was imprisoned for fraud, he became just another in the long list of politicians who found that they were not above the law. Power, the aphrodisiac offered by both politics and money, is also expressed

in the shaping of public opinion which ownership of newspapers, radio stations and television satellites makes possible, so perhaps it is no surprise that many of the world's politicians, from Bottomley and Maxwell to Lord Beaverbrook and Silvio Berlusconi, are linked with the media.

When Charles-Maurice de Talleyrand, who was appointed Bishop of Autun at the age of 35 but renounced the church for politics in 1791, was appointed Foreign Minister of Revolutionary France, he was said to have remarked, *'Je ferai fortune grande, grande fortune'*. This attitude seems to have persisted with politicians of all nations ever since: political power brings financial rewards as cats bring dead birds to the back door. Another of Talleyrand's famous sayings could be applied to the vast body of politicians who have trod the world's stages since then: *'Ils n'ont rien appris, ni rien oublié'* – they have learnt nothing and forgotten nothing. The same ignoble mistakes in pursuit of the same ignoble goals crop up time and again.

Very few politicians who have had to resign their posts have done so because of their political failings. Vice-President Spiro

Agnew, for example, resigned on 10 October 1973 and promptly pleaded 'no contest' to an income tax evasion charge. He was fined a mere $10,000 and placed on three years' probation. The cases of men like Hugh Dalton, who had to resign as Britain's Chancellor of the Exchequer in 1947 when his plan to raise the duty on cigarettes in that year's budget was leaked in a friendly conversation with a journalist on the *Star*, are much rarer than the departures of men like Alan Duncan, whose career as a parliamentary private secretary ended in 1994 when it was disclosed that he had lent money to a neighbour to buy a house from Westminster City Council at a cheap price, and had then bought the house from him. The departures of Michael Heseltine and Leon Brittan from Mrs Thatcher's Cabinet over the Westland helicopter affair were matters of principle – at least more so than the exit of Michael Mates, whose resignation as a Northern Ireland minister was forced because of his friendship with a businessman who had gone into self-imposed exile, Asil Nadir. Such exiles are not rare among politicians either. While it would be unfair to count all those heads of state who have fled their country one step ahead of coup leaders baying for their blood, there are still many like Bettino Craxi, one of Italy's many post-war Prime Ministers, who fled to Tunisia when allegations of corruption became too detailed for his liking.

Most of Japan's post-war Prime Ministers have had to resign in the wake of financial irregularities, from Hitoshi Ashida in 1948 to Morihiro Hosokawa in 1994. The biggest crook of them all, and one of the most effective politicians, was Kakuei Tanaka, whose career spawned a new Japanese phrase, *kinken seiji*, the politics of money and power. Tanaka had been charged with bribery in 1948, just one year after being elected to the Diet, but this did not stop his inexorable rise to the very top, which he reached in 1972. The following year he had a declared taxable income of around £150,000, but it was alleged by a leading political commentator that he had also bought over £300 million worth of stocks and shares during the year, thanks to political contributions effectively culled from leading commercial enterprises that wished to stay in the forefront of the Prime Minister's mind. His downfall finally came when it was shown that he had accepted bribes from the US aircraft manufacturer Lockheed to persuade All Nippon Airways to buy their TriStar jets rather than McDonnell Douglas short-haul jets. The sum involved was said to be about $12 million. After his trial, which was not completed for seven years after Tanaka's arrest, the Justice Minister Akira Hatano gave his opinion: 'Looking for honesty in politicians is like looking for fish in the greengrocer's.' Hatano was himself a politician, of course.

Money can be earned by politicians in many ways. They can take on consultancies (which earned British MPs an estimated £6 million in 1993, in parliamentary consultancies alone); they can sell honours, as Lloyd George did; they can take bribes, or they can write books and articles on any subject that comes to mind. But money is certainly there to be earned. A politician has contacts and influence, and they are things that many people are happy to pay for. Whether it is a lobbyist paying an MP £1,000 to ask a question in the House, or *Tatler* magazine paying the Labour deputy leader John Prescott to write an article, the money would not have been on offer if they had not been who they are, politicians of influence. Sometimes, politicians get carried away with their own sense of importance, which can cause greater difficulties than mere financial ones. House Majority Speaker Newt Gingrich not only signed a book deal worth a reported $4 million with a publishing company owned by Rupert Murdoch, not a politically correct person in America at the time, but also appointed a husband and wife team to act, for $100,000 a year, as his 'personal historians'. Unfortunately it immediately transpired that the wife half of the husband and wife team, Christina Jeffrey, had reportedly once opposed a university course on Holocaust Studies because it was not fair to the Nazis and failed to give the Ku Klux Klan point of view. Mr Gingrich dropped them just as he dropped his fat advance from his publisher, judging it preferable to hang on to the golden goose, his status within the House, even if it meant breaking a few golden eggs.

Politicians are not the only people who spend money unwisely. If one believed all the anecdotes that fly around any government office anywhere in the world, no political activity has ever been undertaken without vast waste of money, but even if one-tenth of what is reported is true, there is a lot of money being thrown away. The case of PowerGen, the newly privatized British electricity generating company, is typical. In 1989 they hosted a party at the Labour Party Conference which cost a reported £30,000, even though the official Labour line was that the company would be renationalized as soon as they returned to power. The following year, not learning from the comparative failure of their first attempt at a party, they hosted their reception in the Imperial Hotel, Blackpool. Unfortunately, the hotel management were at the time involved in an industrial dispute with their staff, and no Labour politician was willing to cross the picket line to come to the party.

Crossing a picket line is a short journey, but a difficult one for many politicians. Other journeys may be longer, but they are easier to make, especially when somebody else is paying. My first encounter with a world leader (one which I am sure he forgot almost as quickly as it had happened) was when I shook hands with Alexei Kosygin, then Soviet Prime Minister, on the steps of his official aircraft at Gander Airport, Newfoundland, in June 1967. He was returning to the Soviet Union after a summit meeting with President Johnson at Glassboro. Five years earlier such a meeting would have been improbable, simply because leaders did not fly about the world in the hectic manner which US Secretary of State Henry Kissinger was to turn into an art form in the 1970s. Five years later it would have been impossible, as security measures would never have allowed a scruffy crowd of long-haired students to surround a leading politician in such insecure surroundings as an airport runway.

At the time of my meeting with Mr Kosygin, I was one of a party of British students travelling to the States for the summer. My trip was largely paid for by my grandmother. With such comparatively early experience in the art of holidaying at somebody else's expense, I should have gone into politics, where free travel is there for the taking. European MEPs spent something approaching £6 million on reclaimable taxi fares in and around Brussels in 1993, to say nothing of travel between the European Parliament and their various constituencies. What is more, these taxi rides were not even

'fact-finding missions', which give politicians the best chance of seeing the world at the taxpayers' expense. It was revealed that 112 MEPs went on a fact-finding mission to the United States in March and April 1986, just a few weeks after another fact-finding mission for 66 MEPs, this time to Swaziland, had cost £345,000. Iain Sproat MP, the British Minister for Sport and a well-known cricket lover, went off to Australia in January 1995 to study the Australian Cricket Academy with a view to shaping government policy on national sports facilities. The fact that England was playing a Test series in Australia at the time was purely coincidental. Times have changed since 1879, when E. J. Reed took on danger and hardship to become the first MP to visit Japan, a fact-finding mission that hardly proved to be a trail blazer for other public servants on the look-out for a good junket. It was another 95 years before a British Prime Minister went there.

Reed went to Japan by sea. These days, as passenger liners are so few and far between that merchant seamen like John Prescott have to find honest work in Parliament, politicians take to the air whenever the opportunity arises. The coachman employed by Sir George Cayley MP was the first man in Britain to get off the ground in a heavier than air machine, a feat that was accomplished in a glider of Sir George's construction in 1853, half a century before the Wright brothers' first powered flight. Since then, politicians have taken to the air with eagerness. Ramsay MacDonald was the first Prime Minister to fly, and when Neville Chamberlain went to Munich in 1938 to meet Hitler, it was a sensation that he travelled by air. It was also a great ordeal for a man approaching 70 who was far more at home on the water, as was proven by the fact that he once saved a girl from drowning. Flying was not really established for politicians until after the war, and even then it was dangerous. T. L. Horabin MP was badly injured in an air crash at Stowting, near Folkestone, on 12 January 1947 when a BOAC Dakota came down in dreadful weather. Six of his fellow passengers were killed. American Presidents never fly by public transport: they use Air Force One, which in Roosevelt's time was known as 'The Sacred Cow'. President Carter's aircraft was nicknamed 'Peanuts One'.

Hugh Gaitskell, Labour Party leader from 1955 until his death in 1963, had the knack of being in the wrong place at the wrong time. In October 1950 he was in North America when Sir Stafford Cripps announced his resignation as Chancellor. Prime Minister Attlee's offer of the Chancellorship, and Gaitskell's acceptance, were relayed by transatlantic cable. Just over six years later, Gaitskell was once again in America, this time on a lecturing tour, when Sir Anthony Eden resigned as Prime Minister. Gaitskell had to cut short his tour and rush back to London to face the new Prime Minister, Harold Macmillan, across the floor of the House of Commons. Macmillan had not had to leave the country to take up his new job, as one of his predecessors, Herbert Asquith had done. In April 1908, when Asquith succeeded the dying Henry Campbell-Bannerman as leader of the Liberal Party, and thus as Prime Minister, King Edward VII was on holiday in Biarritz. Asquith therefore had to travel to the South of France, and on 8 April in the Hôtel du Palais, Biarritz, Asquith kissed the King's hand on his appointment as Prime Minister.

Kissing hands is the ultimate ambition for a British politician, but many of them put in many long hours of practice for this accolade by kissing other parts of many other people's bodies. The inevitable result is that sexual scandals among politicians are these days so commonplace that they can hardly be described as curiosities. In 1963 the Conservative Government was dealt its death blow by the Profumo affair, which had everything the prurient public could ask for: sex, lies and espionage. The entire career of President Clinton has been dogged by allegations of infidelities, but these days we seem to expect so much more moral rectitude in our leaders than in the past. Franklin D. Roosevelt, partly paralysed by polio, apparently made use of two strong Secret Service agents to

lift him onto his mistress, and, if we are to believe all the rumours, John F. Kennedy had affairs with most of the women he met. Antoine Pinay, formerly the French Prime Minister, was being widely canvassed as a presidential candidate in 1965, but dropped out of the race following allegations that large bribes had been offered to him to stand for the presidency, and that details of his private life would be made public if he refused. He did refuse, but the allegations were not made public, perhaps because in refusing to run for the top job, Pinay had effectively ended his political career anyway. A later French President, François Mitterrand, not only admitted to fathering an illegitimate daughter but also found his links with the wartime Vichy regime in France being given an exhaustive airing. This did far less damage to his political career than the gift of diamonds from 'Emperor' Bokassa did to his predecessor Valéry Giscard d'Estaing, proving that girls, rather than diamonds, are a politician's best friend.

Illegitimate children seem to be an occupational hazard of politics. Fathering (or, on some occasions, mothering) children out of wedlock seems to have little bearing on a politician's ability to do the job he or she was elected for, but for some reason the general public expects different standards in its leaders. Now that almost one-third of children born in Britain are born out of wedlock, it seems churlish to worry about any politician who has produced at least two-thirds of his offspring within the confines of marriage, but that still leaves several Members of Parliament operating well above the national average. In other parts of the world, the same problem arises, although the most spectacular example is probably that of the right-wing Russian politician Vladimir Zhirinovsky (leader of Russia's Liberal Democrats, who like the Japanese version are neither liberal nor democratic). Zhirinovsky claimed in 1994 that it was the duty of every Russian woman of child-bearing age to have a child, and that he personally would set about fathering as many of them as he possibly could. There may be something lost in the translation, but what a noted political commentator has called Mr Zhirinovsky's 'weak grip on sanity' leads one to suspect he has not been wildly mis-translated. There have been no reports as yet that queues of women waiting to be serviced by Mr Zhirinovsky have stretched from Moscow to the Urals.

SUPPLEMENTARIES

Prime Minister fails to pay electricity bill:

Edouard Balladur, PM of France, had the electricity cut off in his Deauville residence when he failed to pay an electricity bill amounting to FF1,816 (about £200), January 1995.

Prime Minister defaces Rubens painting:

During the Second World War Winston Churchill decided that a mouse in a large Rubens painting in the Great Hall of Chequers was not visible, so he touched up the picture to make the mouse more evident. When the painting was loaned to a London gallery for exhibition, it was cleaned and the Churchillian mouse removed.

Future Prime Minister arrested by NKVD:

Harold Wilson, taking a photograph on behalf of Prime Minister Winston Churchill in Moscow in 1954, unfortunately included the Lubyanka Prison in the background, which resulted in his detention for an hour by the NKVD, later the KGB.

Sinn Fein leaders claim income support:

Gerry Adams, MP for West Belfast from 1983 to 1992, claimed £53.65 a week income support during 1994.

Martin McGuinness, leader of Sinn Fein's peace talks delegation, claimed £72.96 a week income support and unemployment benefit during 1994.

Cabinet Minister forced to resign after three in a bed allegations during a divorce trial:

Sir Charles Dilke, 1885

Politicians forced to resign after allegations of sexual impropriety:

Gary Hart, Democratic Senator from Colorado, forced out of the 1988 presidential race after allegations of an affair with Donna Rice.

David Mellor, Conservative MP for Putney and Heritage Secretary, after allegations of an affair with Antonia de Sancha, September 1992.

Cecil Parkinson, Conservative MP for Hertsmere and Secretary of State for Trade and Industry, after admitting an affair with Sarah Keays, October 1983.

John Profumo, Conservative MP for Stratford-upon-Avon and Secretary of State for War, after misleading the House over his relationship with Christine Keeler, June 1963.

Timothy Yeo, Conservative MP for Suffolk South and Minister with Responsibility for the Countryside, after admitting fathering an illegitimate child, January 1994.

7 KEEPING IT IN THE FAMILY

Politicians are human beings, and they have to try to live their own lives at the same time as trying to change everybody else's. They are born, they marry, they become parents, they have their good days and their bad days, and then they die. This is not a curiosity, this is the way life works. The fact that politicians appear to get involved in more scandals, sexual peccadilloes and financial irregularities than the rest of us is not surprising either: their lives are more in the spotlight than those in most other sectors of the community, and there is more public interest in the adulterous affairs of a Cabinet Minister than of, say, a newspaper editor. Sleaze is not a curiosity, nor even a political 'factor': it happens everywhere, but most of us are lucky enough not to have every move we make spread across the pages of a newspaper, nor to have every word we say, however unguarded, recorded by a thousand microphones.

The first significant thing that happens to a person after birth is being given a name. For a politician, the name you live with is very important. Politicians tend, in all cultures, to use the name they were given at birth as the name they are known by in politics, although there have always been exceptions, especially among those politicians not very democratically elected. The Soviet revolutionaries Lenin, Trotsky and Stalin were born Vladimir Ilyich Ulyanov, Lev Davidovitch Bronstein and Joseph Vissarionovich Djugashvili respectively, but needed names that would reflect their revolutionary fervour, as well as trip rather more easily off the tongue. Vyacheslav Scriabin changed his name to Molotov (meaning 'hammer') for the less noble purpose of staying one step ahead of the tsarist police. Or maybe he guessed that a 'Scriabin Cocktail' would sound less threatening.

John Major's brother is Terry Major-Ball, and one can understand why a politician such as Mr Major decided to use only half the possible surname options open to him. Even when the news for his party was good, for example if his opinion poll rating rose, the headline writers would still be able to state accurately, 'Major-Ball's Up', which is not the image a Prime Minister likes to project. It is not only Conservative politicians who change their surnames for political reasons, however. Ann Clwyd, the Labour MP for Cynon Valley and Opposition spokeswoman on employment, was born Ann Lewis and on her marriage in 1963 became Ann Roberts. Clwyd is probably more memorable and more Welsh than either of her actual surnames. It is certainly more difficult to spell.

Lord David Sutch is perhaps the only would-be politician to ennoble himself by deed poll while trying to get into Parliament, although several politicians have renounced their inherited peerages in order to remain in the House of Commons. Anthony Wedgwood Benn became briefly Viscount Stansgate in 1961, and it was his action in standing at the by-election caused by his own ennoblement, and winning it, that brought about the change in the law that allowed titles to be renounced. Benn has gone further, by renouncing half of his surname (like John Major) and also half of his first name, so that he is now known as the determinedly egalitarian Tony Benn. Other nobles to have renounced their titles for political reasons include Lord Hailsham (Quintin Hogg), the 14th Earl of Home (Sir Alec Douglas-Home) and Lord James Douglas-Hamilton, who in 1994 renounced his right to inherit his uncle's title, even though it was probable that he had no claim on it anyway.

Parents of budding politicians have a great responsibility when it comes to choosing a name for their child. A former Prime Minister of Swaziland – a position which, it must be admitted, holds rather more status than power – presumably had parents who could not quite decide whether to eliminate all European influences from his name. To Anglo-Saxon ears, at any rate, his full name of Prince Mabandla Ndawombili Fred Dlamini does not strike awe into the heart. Joseph-Désiré Mobutu, President of Zaïre, changed his name in January 1972 to Mobutu Sese Seko Kuku Ngbendu wa Za

Banga, a name which apparently tells more of his manly prowess and great political skills than the less macho and far more colonial Joseph-Désiré could ever hope to do. President Bongo, leader of Gabon from 1967, when he was but a stripling of 31, has also given up his French forename Albert-Bernard and is now known to his closest friends as Omar, although his subjects still call him 'Mr President' or 'Sir' or whatever he wants to be called.

There do not seem to be any particular names that go with political power. The only surnames that have cropped up more than once for American Presidents are Adams, Harrison, Roosevelt and Johnson, and of these, only the Johnsons, Andrew and Lyndon, were not related. A third unrelated Johnson, Richard, was Vice-President to Martin Van Buren between 1837 and 1841. George Clinton was Vice-President to Thomas Jefferson and James Madison, and Bill Clinton (born Blythe and only an adopted Clinton) has been President since 1993. There have been no Smiths, Jones, Browns or Greens, the most common Anglo-Saxon surnames, presiding in the Oval Office yet, just as there have been no Smiths, Jones, Browns or Greens in Number 10 Downing Street. Alfred E. Smith and Joseph T. Robinson were the plainly named Democratic presidential ticket in 1928, but they lost out to Hoover and Curtis. John Smith has led the British Labour Party, George Brown has been their deputy leader, Helmut Schmidt has been Chancellor of Germany and Albert Lebrun was President of France from 1932 to 1940, but the nearest to such a commonplace surname reaching the peak of British politics was when the 14th Earl of Derby, Sir Edward Geoffry Smith-Stanley, held office three times between 1852 and 1868.

The only surname that has made its way to both the White House and Number 10 is Wilson. Woodrow Wilson was President from 1913 to 1921, and Harold Wilson was Prime Minister four times between 1964 and 1976. Henry Wilson, Ulysses S. Grant's second Vice-President, became in 1875 the fifth Vice-President to die in office. There have been two different President Amins in recent years. Idi Amin ruled Uganda until he was overthrown on 11 April 1979, and just five months later, the Soviets installed Hafizullah Amin as President of the Revolutionary Council in Afghanistan. In France, Alexandre Millerand was President from 1920 to 1924; and 57 years later, the same name with the t's crossed moved into the Elysée Palace when François Mitterrand became President.

Politicians, once they decide what to call themselves, are sent to school like the rest of us. Some children know from a very early age that they want to go into politics. Harold Wilson was photographed by his father on the steps of Number 10 Downing Street when he was still in short trousers; William

Hague, Conservative MP for Richmond, Yorkshire, from 1989, spoke at the Conservative Party Conference at Blackpool in 1977 aged 16; and a five-year-old Franklin Delano Roosevelt met President Cleveland at the White House in 1887. Cleveland said to him, 'I've made a strange wish for you. It is that you may never be President of the United States.' Like most wishes, it did not come true.

Some schools are better than others at breeding politicians. In Britain, seven Prime Ministers have been educated at Harrow, the most recent being Sir Winston Churchill, four have been educated at Westminster and 19 at Eton, the most recent being Sir Alec Douglas-Home. Twenty-five of our 52 Prime Ministers went up to Oxford University, and 13 to Cambridge. John Major is only the third Conservative leader this century not to have had an Oxbridge education, and the only one since Disraeli to have had no formal tertiary education at all. James Callaghan and Ramsay MacDonald are the only Labour Prime Ministers without the benefit of a university education.

Once a politician grows up, he or she will, like most other human beings, fall in love. Many of the problems experienced by Western politicians in recent years can be put down to the fact that power is a strong aphrodisiac. Look at Henry Kissinger – he is nobody's idea of a Mr Universe, but it seemed that his years of shuttle diplomacy as Secretary of State to President Nixon were just an excuse to be seen at a vast range of official banquets or clambering down the steps of a jumbo jet with another stunning lady on his arm. All too few leading politicians over the years have remained unmarried, but Mr Kissinger made the most of his years as the world's most powerful bachelor.

Being married is seen as a political advantage in most societies, and as a political necessity in many. James Buchanan, US President from 1857 to 1861, is the only President to have been unmarried, and Ronald Reagan the only one to have been divorced. When Mrs Thatcher became British Prime Minister in 1979, her triumph was viewed in male-dominated Japanese society as something of a surprise, but they could believe anything to be possible in a society where a decade earlier an unmarried man, Edward Heath, had made it to the top, the first unmarried Prime Minister Britain had had since Arthur Balfour almost 70 years earlier. Heath's success was, to the Japanese, a far more amazing achievement than that of Mrs Thatcher. Not that in Japan a married life is necessarily a recipe for lifelong happiness, but a wife is a necessary appendage for any man who wants to be seen to be conforming in that most conformist of nations. When Eisaku Sato, Japanese Prime Minister from 1964 to 1972, confessed in a women's magazine article to beating his wife from time to time, it caused no particular uproar in Japan. Wives are there to be beaten, after all. Only when the article was reprinted abroad did the fuss begin. One of Japan's many scandal-ridden leaders of more recent times, Sosuke Uno, was forced to resign because of his relationship with a geisha. It was not the fact that he had a mistress for many years that was the problem; it was the fact that he was unable to stop her telling all to the tabloid Press when he decided to end the relationship. The Japanese newspapers did not cry, as the British ones so hypocritically do, 'How can we have a leader who has a mistress?' Their message was 'How can we have a leader who cannot handle his mistress well enough to stop her spilling the beans?'

But politics is power, and power is something we all like to keep in the family. The great royal houses of the world grew up because the dominant political leader of the time (which generally meant the dominant military leader, though not always) wanted to retain for his family the trappings of power that he had accumulated for himself. Mere commoners are no different. Some have even tried to turn themselves into royalty, but the most recent example of this lust for glory, by Jean-Bedel Bokassa of the Central African Republic, failed. Bokassa decreed himself Emperor Bokassa I of the Central African Empire in December 1976. Within three years, however, he had been overthrown, and all of his family with him – except those that Bokassa himself had put to death in the years of his glory.

Political families are the norm rather than a curiosity. Think of the Kennedys, the Stevensons and even the Bush family in America. Think of the Churchills, the Chamberlains and the Bonham-Carters in Britain, the Gandhis in India or the Bandaranaikes in Sri Lanka. Politics is as much a family business as owning a factory or being doctors or teachers for generation after generation. Yet even within the political family structure, there are some who stand out. Benjamin Harrison signed the United States Declaration of Independence. His son William became President, as did his great-grandson, another Benjamin. His grandson, John Scott Harrison, had to be content with just being a Congressman.

Nicholas Soames, Conservative MP for Crawley and son of the late Sir Christopher Soames, is also the grandson of Sir Winston Churchill and the great-grandson of Randolph Churchill. All four men have held government office. Nicholas Soames was also personal assistant to US Senator Mark Hatfield for two years in the 1970s, so his experience, both inherited and learnt, of the workings of government on both sides of the Atlantic would take some beating. However, the Soames family record of four generations in government has been equalled in Britain by the Goschen family. When the 4th Viscount Goschen was appointed a junior minister at the Department of Transport in 1992, at the age of 26, he became the fourth generation of his family to hold government office, and all of them did so in the twentieth century. Between 1863 and 1900 George Joachim Goschen was variously MP for the City of London, Liverpool, Ripon and Edinburgh, ending his career as Liberal Unionist Member for St George's Hanover Square. He succeeded Lord Randolph Churchill as Chancellor of the Exchequer in 1886 and served as First Lord of the Admiralty from 1895 to 1900. He was then created the 1st Viscount Goschen. His son, also George Joachim, was an MP from 1895, and was appointed parliamentary secretary to the Board of Agriculture in 1918. The 3rd Viscount Goschen had a less invigorating political career, but the 4th Viscount, named Giles John Harry rather than George Joachim, maintained the tradition by becoming, on his appointment in 1992, the first government minister to be born in the Wilson–Heath era.

In politics, it seems to be the brothers who are the problem. President Jimmy Carter had to put up with the embarrassments of his hard-drinking brother Billy, who did most things from advertising beer to consorting with Colonel Gaddafi, and President Bill Clinton had the complication of his half-brother Roger, who has a history of dealing drugs and making terrible rock records. In 1995 Roger was even invited to sing at a sports festival in North Korea, a regime as opposed to the American way of life as ever Libya was in President Carter's day. President Eisenhower, on the other hand, had six brothers, and they all behaved themselves properly. John Major has an elder brother, Terry Major-Ball, whose only interesting facet is that he makes his young brother seem exciting. Mrs Thatcher, blessed with only a sister, has not had to put up with sibling revelations in every tabloid.

Sometimes brothers both take up politics, like the Tory MPs Sir Patrick and the late Sir Robert McNair-Wilson, but when this happens, one usually outshines the other. Rajiv Gandhi, son of Indira Gandhi and grandson of Jawaharlal Nehru, became the third generation in his family to lead India, but only because of family pressure for him to enter politics after the death of his younger brother Sanjay in an air crash. Austen and Neville Chamberlain were half-brothers, sons of Joseph Chamberlain, but it was the younger brother Neville who became Prime Minister, while Austen had to be content with the Chancellorship of the Exchequer. The only brothers who both became Prime Minister of a major elected democracy in recent times are Nobusuke Kishi and Eisaku Sato of Japan. Kishi, the elder, was Prime Minister from 1957 to 1960, and Sato, the younger brother who was adopted into another branch of the family, was Japan's longest-serving postwar leader, from 1964 to 1972.

John F. Kennedy was the means by which his father, Joseph Kennedy, fulfilled his political ambitions only because his elder brother, Joseph Jnr, had been killed in a wartime plane crash. JFK appointed his brother Robert as Attorney-General, despite his past association with Wisconsin Senator Joseph McCarthy

and his virulently right-wing UnAmerican Activities Committee, on whose staff Bobby Kennedy served in 1953. His youngest brother, Senator Edward Kennedy, had become by 1994 a senator of 32 years' standing, one of the four longest-serving senators in Washington. Edward's son Patrick was elected, for Rhode Island, as the youngest member of the House of Representatives; his nephew Joseph P. Kennedy II retained his Boston congressional seat; and his brother-in-law Sargent Shriver had stood unsuccessfully for the Vice-Presidency on the George McGovern ticket in 1972. By the time Rose Kennedy died in 1995, aged 104, another grandson, Mark Kennedy Shriver, had made it to the Maryland State Congress, and granddaughter Kathleen was Lieutenant-Governor of the same state.

George Bush's two sons, George Jnr and Jeb, both ran for Governorships in 1994, but while George was successful in Texas, Jeb just failed to take Florida. Charles Robb, son-in-law of President Lyndon B. Johnson, held on to his Senate seat in Virginia. Robb, an ex-captain in the Marines, is one of the few Senators to have been married at the White House, where his wedding to Lynda Bird Johnson took place in December 1967. Johnson's other daughter, Luci Baines, was also married during her father's time in office. David Eisenhower, grandson of President Eisenhower and the person after whom Camp David, the presidential retreat, is named, married Julie Nixon, daughter of Eisenhower's Vice-President Richard Nixon, but that ceremony did not take place at the White House. The only President to get married for the first time while in office is Grover Cleveland, who married the 21-year-old Frances Folsom in 1886, when he was 49. Cleveland had been in trouble during the 1884 election campaign for having fathered a child by 'a promiscuous lady of Buffalo', giving rise to the campaign chant, 'Where's your pa? Gone to the White House, ha ha ha.' He was also accused of being an early draft dodger, managing to avoid service during the Civil War by staying on at his job as a lawyer in Buffalo and hiring another man to take his place in the army. This was all quite true, but as his opponent James Blaine was accused of the same offence, it did not affect Cleveland's prospects of election. The nation knew it was not going to be led by a military man, whoever won.

The family connections in politics are everywhere. Franklin Delano Roosevelt was Theodore Roosevelt's fifth cousin and, more intriguingly, recent biographical research in Canada shows that he was also related to Winston Churchill. Three family lines linked, through Churchill's American mother, making them seventh cousins once removed, eighth cousins once removed and eighth cousins twice removed. The Hon. Hester Grenville, later Baroness Chatham, was the wife, the sister, the mother and the aunt of four Prime Ministers, while Balfour was Lord Salisbury's nephew. Lord Salisbury's son,

Lord Robert Cecil, was an MP from 1906 and Stanley Baldwin's son, Oliver, was Labour MP for Dudley from 1929 to 1931, but was never a Member while his Conservative father was in office. Stanley Baldwin had in his turn taken over his Bewdley seat from his father, who had died in 1908. Megan Lloyd George, daughter of the man who knew my father, was a long-serving Liberal Member of Parliament. Jo Grimond, leader of the Liberal Party from 1956 to 1967, married Asquith's granddaughter, while the Conservative Cabinet Minister Nicholas Ridley was a nephew by marriage of Jo Grimond's sister Cressida. Another Conservative Minister, Virginia Bottomley, has left-of-centre family connections. She is the niece of Douglas Jay, Labour Cabinet Minister of the 1960s, and thus also related by marriage to the Labour Prime Minister James Callaghan. Winston Churchill's son, son-in-law and two grandsons have all been Conservative MPs, while Peter Brooke, Heritage Secretary and former Northern Ireland Secretary, is the son of the late Henry Brooke, Home Secretary to both Harold Macmillan and Sir Alec Douglas-Home.

Husbands and wives occasionally go into business together, but most cases of both halves of a marriage going into politics are not simultaneous but consecutive. The first woman to take her seat in the House of Commons, Lady Astor, was elected because her husband succeeded to the title of Viscount Astor in 1919, and had to resign the seat at Plymouth (Sutton) which he had held since 1910. When John Golding resigned as Labour MP for Newcastle-under-Lyme in 1986, his place was taken by his second wife, Llinos, who had until then been his secretary and assistant. When Lord Apsley was killed in an air crash in the Middle East in 1943, his widow stood in the by-election at Bristol Central, and actually increased his majority. During the war, the Labour Party had undertaken not to oppose Conservative-held seats at by-elections, but no fewer than seven independent candidates stood against Lady Apsley, one being described as 'President of the Society of Angelic Revelations'. Under the circumstances, it was surprising her majority was as high as 1,559.

Wives have in recent years stood in for dead husbands quite regularly, from Corazon Aquino in the Philippines and Isabelita Perón in Argentina to Mrs Sirimavo Bandaranaike in Sri Lanka and Begum Khaleda Zia in Bangladesh. When Representative Larry P. McDonald was killed in the 1983 KAL jumbo jet disaster, his wife Kathryn tried to run for his congressional seat, but failed to win nomination. Married couples in politics together are more rare, but when Aneurin Bevan married Jennie Lee in 1934, both were already Labour MPs, Bevan for Ebbw Vale and Miss Lee for North Lanark. Virginia and Peter Bottomley, Nicholas and Anne Winterton, Gwyneth and John Dunwoody, and Gordon and Bridget Prentice are recent examples of married couples in Parliament together, but togetherness seems to work better for Conservatives than for Labour. The Tory Bottomleys and Wintertons are still together, but the pressures of Commons life told on the Socialist Dunwoodys and Prentices, who have split up.

Overseas, they do things differently. Chairman Mao was the Great Helmsman of China, but his wife Jiang Qing did most to help run the ship of state on to the rocks. Bill Clinton did not finally appoint his wife Hillary to his Cabinet, but he gave her the job of trying to sort out the labyrinthine problems of health care. His Republican opponent in Congress,

Newt Gingrich, knows how to deal with difficult or unnecessary wives. He served divorce papers on his first wife while she was in hospital recovering from a cancer operation. He commented: 'She's not young enough or pretty enough to be the wife of a President. Besides she has cancer.' It remains to be seen whether the second Mrs Gingrich will become the wife of a President. South African President Nelson Mandela, who was incidentally born Rolihlahla Mandela and only took the forename Nelson when he attended a mission school, had both support and problems from his second wife Winnie during his 27 years in prison. The marriage did not long outlast his release, but his political marriage problems are nothing compared with those of Alberto Fujimori.

The trouble started for Señor Fujimori, President of Peru, when his wife Susana moved out of the Presidential Palace in August 1994 and gave up her official role as First Lady in an attempt to oust her husband from the very top job. President Fujimori had in July of that year passed a law that prohibits close relatives of the serving President from standing for office, but that did not stop his wife. She reverted to her maiden name of Susana Higuchi and formed her own party, the ineptly named Harmony 21st Century Party, with which she intended to show her husband anything but harmony. However, she then came up against another remarkably useful Peruvian law which states that any new party has to show that it has at least 100,000 supporters before it can take part in the political process. The Harmony 21st Century Party duly produced a list of 147,000 signatures, but the electoral board managed to prove that over 135,000 of these were fakes or otherwise invalid. It seemed that President Fujimori was winning the battle against his wife, who was reduced to complaining to the Organization of American States that she was being denied her constitutional right, as an adult over the age of 35, to stand for office.

In October 1993 the Greek Prime Minister Andreas Papandreou made his wife Mimi director of his office, and it would be unsporting to suggest that she, being his long-time mistress and third wife, knew what politicians can sometimes get up to and wanted to be able to control his day. While he was at it, Papandreou made his son George Deputy Foreign Minister, his wife's cousin George Liani Deputy Culture Minister and his doctor Dimitris Kremastinos Health Minister. In November 1937, Paulina Zhemchugina, wife of Soviet Foreign Minister Vyacheslav Molotov, was promoted from the heady position of Chief of the Soviet Union's Soap and Scent Trust to being Vice-Commissar for the Food Industry. She thereafter attended Cabinet meetings with her husband.

Sometimes politics seems to skip a generation, as with Benito Mussolini and his granddaughter Alessandra, neo-Fascist MP for Naples and coincidentally daughter of Sophia

Loren's sister Maria. The skipping of a generation may in part be because Il Duce ordered the execution of his son-in-law Count Galeazzo Ciano, who was at one time Italy's Foreign Minister. That sort of thing tends to put a family off politics. Similarly, the suicide of Prince Fumimaro Konoye, Japan's Prime Minister from 1937 to 1939 and again in 1941, just before his arrest as a war criminal, seems to have deterred his immediate heirs from following in their father's footsteps. However, his grandson Morihiro Hosokawa became Prime Minister in August 1993, although he only lasted for eight months in the top job.

Family ties are still the most important connections you can make in politics. Political families still grow, especially in Britain, despite French Prime Minister Mme Edith Cresson's assertion in an interview that one quarter of American, British and German men are homosexual, and that 'Anglo-Saxon men are not interested in women'. The track record of too many male politicians would tend to prove her wrong.

SUPPLEMENTARIES

British Prime Ministers since 1900 who changed their names before becoming Prime Minister:

Lord Salisbury, born 1830 as Lord Robert Cecil, became Viscount Cranborne in 1865, and became 3rd Marquess of Salisbury in 1868.

Sir Henry Campbell-Bannerman, born Henry Campbell in 1836, was known as Henry Campbell-Bannerman from 1872.

Lord Home, born 1903 as the Hon. Alexander Frederick Douglas-Home, known as Lord Dunglass from 1918 and as the 14th Earl of Home from 1951. He renounced his title while Prime Minister, to become Sir Alec Douglas-Home.

Margaret Thatcher, born Margaret Roberts 1925, married Denis

Thatcher in 1951.

American Presidents since 1900 who changed their names before taking office:

Gerald Ford, born 1913 as Leslie King, changed his name to Gerald R. Ford when legally adopted as a young child by his mother's second husband.

William Clinton, born William Jefferson Blythe in 1946, changed his name in 1962 to Clinton, his stepfather's name.

American Presidents who were married twice:

John Tyler, firstly to Letitia Christian (married 1813, she died 1842), secondly to Julia Gardiner (married 1844, during Tyler's presidency).

Millard Fillmore, firstly to Abigail Powers (married 1826, she died 1853), secondly to Caroline McIntosh (married 1858).

Benjamin Harrison, firstly to Caroline Scott (married 1852, she died 1892 as First Lady), secondly to Mary Dimmick (married 1896).

Theodore Roosevelt, firstly to Alice Lee (married 1880, she died 1884), secondly to Edith Carow (married 1886).

Woodrow Wilson, firstly to Ellen Axson (married 1885, she died 1914, as First Lady), secondly to Edith Galt (married 1915, during Wilson's presidency).

Ronald Reagan, firstly to Jane Wyman (married 1940, divorced 1948), secondly to Nancy Davis (married 1952).

British Prime Ministers who were married twice:

Sir Robert Walpole, firstly to Catherine Shorter (married 1700, she died 1717), secondly to Maria Skerrett (married 1738, while Prime Minister).

Duke of Grafton, firstly to the Hon. Anne Liddell (married 1765, divorced 1769), secondly to Elizabeth Wrottesley (married 1769).

Lord Shelburne, firstly to Lady Sophia Carerett (married 1765, she died 1771), secondly to Lady Louisa FitzPatrick (married 1779).

Henry Addington, firstly to Ursula Hammond (married 1781, she died 1811), secondly to the Hon. Mrs Marianne Townshend (married 1823).

Earl of Liverpool, firstly to Lady Louisa Hervey (married 1795, she died 1821), secondly to Mary Chester (married 1822, while Prime Minister).

Lord John Russell, firstly to Adelaide, Baroness Ribblesdale (married 1835, she died 1838), secondly to Lady Frances Elliott-Murray-Kynynmound (married 1841).

Earl of Aberdeen, firstly to Lady Catherine Hamilton (married 1805, she died 1812), secondly to Harriet, Viscountess Hamilton (married 1815).

Herbert Asquith, firstly to Helen Melland (married 1877, she died 1891), secondly to Emma Tennant (married 1894).

David Lloyd George, firstly to Margaret Owen (married 1888, she died 1941), secondly to Frances Stevenson (married 1943).

Sir Anthony Eden, firstly to Beatrice Beckett (married 1923, divorced 1950), secondly to Anne Spencer-Churchill (married 1952).

Politicians who did not use their first forename:

Jeremy John Durham (Paddy) Ashdown, Leader of the British Liberal Democrats

Linden Forbes Sampson Burnham, Prime Minister of Guyana

Leonard James Callaghan, Prime Minister of the UK

Arthur Neville Chamberlain, Prime Minister of the UK

Joseph Austen Chamberlain, Foreign Secretary of the UK

Charles Joseph Clark, Prime Minister of Canada

Stephen Grover Cleveland, President of the US

John Calvin Coolidge, President of the US

Sir Robert Anthony Eden, Prime Minister of the UK

John Malcolm Fraser, Prime Minister of Australia

John Selwyn Brooke Lloyd, Speaker of the House of Commons, 1971–6

James Ramsay MacDonald, Prime Minister of the UK

Edward Gough Whitlam, Prime Minister of Australia

James Harold Wilson, Prime Minister of the UK

Thomas Woodrow Wilson, President of the US

Politicians' wives who did not use their first forename:

Eleanor Rosalynn Carter, wife of US President Jimmy Carter

Claudia Alta (Lady Bird) Johnson, wife of US President Lyndon B. Johnson

Thelma Catherine Patricia Nixon, wife of US President Richard Nixon

Anne Frances (Nancy) Reagan, wife of US President Ronald Reagan

Anna Eleanor Roosevelt, wife of US President Franklin Delano Roosevelt

Prime Ministers educated at Eton and Christ Church, Oxford:

Sir Alec Douglas-Home, Sir Anthony Eden, Lord Rosebery, Lord Salisbury, William Gladstone, Lord Derby, George Canning, Lord Grenville, Lord Portland, the Hon. George Grenville

THE END OF THE DEBATE

As the nineteenth century finally yielded to the twentieth, America's President McKinley gave his official approval to the establishment of a Pan-American Exposition, to be held in Buffalo, New York State. The Exposition was to show off the huge advances in science and civilization that America had enjoyed since the end of the Civil War, and Thomas Edison's cinematograph company was granted the exclusive rights to film the whole thing. President McKinley himself came to the Exposition on 6 September 1901, and was filmed by the Edison Company making a speech. While the cameramen were changing their reels and waiting for the President to re-emerge from the Temple of Music, word came that he had been shot. The Edison Company had missed the scoop of

the still very young century, but they were able to film the crowd's reaction to the news, as well as the funeral procession when the President died eight days later. They also wanted to film the execution of the assassin, Leon Czolgosz, but were refused permission. So they staged a reconstruction for the cameras, the first known example of that now common news practice of staging events for the cameras as though they were real or spontaneous. The violent death of a politician is big news.

Czolgosz, incidentally, was executed (in, but not on, camera) on 29 October 1901, only 45 days after the death of McKinley. This was a quicker judicial death than the only other presidential assassin to be tried for his crime, Charles J. Guiteau, who shot President Garfield on 2 July 1881. Garfield lingered on until 19 September before dying of a combination of his wounds and poor medical care, which was bad luck for both Garfield and Guiteau, who was subsequently hanged. The other two successful presidential killers, or alleged killers, John Wilkes Booth and Lee Harvey Oswald, both died within 12 days of their crimes but without either of them having stood trial or even having had a chance to answer the allegations.

Assassination has always been used as a rapid way of effecting political change, and politicians have to get used to bodyguards and the threat of physical attack. Most assassination attempts are unsuccessful, with at least six American Presidents over the past 150 years surviving attacks, as against four who have succumbed. Although Lincoln, Garfield, McKinley and Kennedy are remembered as victims, others from Theodore Roosevelt to Bill Clinton have survived attempts on their lives of varying competence. America's seventh President, Andrew

Jackson, survived an attack by an Englishman named Richard Lawrence, who believed that he was the rightful heir to the thrones of both Britain and America, and only Jackson stood in his way. Lawrence pointed his two pistols at Jackson, and fired at point-blank range, but both misfired and Jackson was shocked but unhurt.

Former President Theodore Roosevelt was shot in October 1912 by John F. Schrank, when he was about to deliver a campaign speech, aiming to get back to the White House he had left in 1909. Schrank, who claimed he had been told to kill Roosevelt by the ghost of McKinley (a defence which did not work), hit him in the chest, but the bullet was deflected from the heart by Roosevelt's spectacles case and by his speech, which was folded up in his inside pocket. It was clearly a very long speech, to take up enough paper to deflect a bullet, and Roosevelt insisted on delivering it before receiving medical attention. This he did, and although he lived for another seven years, none of them were as President. The campaign speech had saved his life, but not his election prospects.

His fifth cousin, Franklin Delano Roosevelt, who incidentally holds the record for both the shortest full term as President (3 years 322 days from 4 March 1933 to 20 January 1937) and the longest total time as President (12 years 39 days from 4 March 1933 to 12 April 1945), was almost assassinated before his inauguration. In Miami in February 1933, Giuseppe Zangara fired shots at the President-elect, but hit Anton Cermak, Mayor of Chicago, killing him and wounding several others. Roosevelt was unharmed. On 1 November 1950, a Puerto Rican attempted to shoot President Harry S. Truman when he appeared at the window of Blair House, where he was living temporarily while the White House roof was being repaired. President Reagan was shot and wounded by John Hinckley in Washington on 30 March 1981, but he survived to serve his full eight years, the first President elected in a year ending in a zero not to die in office since the fifth President, James Monroe, who won the 1820 election. In the intervening 160 years, seven Presidents elected in years ending in a zero had all died in office. William Harrison, elected in 1840, set the trend by making a speech which lasted an hour and three quarters during his inauguration on 4 March 1841, which was an uncommonly cold day. This speech was the longest ever made before or since by a new President, and however brilliant it may have been, such long exposure to the elements caused the 68-year-old Harrison to catch a cold which developed into pneumonia, from which he died one month later. John Tyler, his Vice-President who became known as 'His Accidency' when he succeeded to the Presidency, was almost killed himself in 1844 when he visited the frigate *Princeton* with his Secretary of State, Abel P. Upshur. An explosion killed the unfortunate Upshur, but the President was unharmed. The Presidents elected in 1860 (Lincoln), 1880 (Garfield) and 1900 (McKinley) were assassinated, while Warren Harding, elected in 1920, died mired in scandal on 2 August 1923. F. D. Roosevelt was elected in 1940, as he had been in 1932 and 1936 and would be again in 1944, but he died in office in 1945. Kennedy was elected in 1960. Strangely, only one other President, Zachary Taylor in 1850, has ever died in office.

President Johnson was frequently the target of Vietnam War protesters, but although his car was spattered with paint (red and white glossy thrown at his motorcade in Melbourne,

Australia, in 1965, for example) and his bodyguards had to deal with the full larder of eggs, flour and milk in missile form, he was never the subject of a serious assassination attempt. President Clinton was the focus in late 1994 of many curious events which could probably be described as attempts on his life, but which were more likely to have been publicity stunts or deliberate suicides. On 12 September a 38-year-old man crashed a stolen Cessna light aircraft on the South Lawn of the White House, just below the Clintons' bedroom, killing himself but harming nobody else. President and Mrs Clinton were not at the White House at the time. The security surrounding the White House, including Stinger anti-aircraft missiles on the roof, was not activated. Six weeks later, on 29 October, a 26-year-old from Colorado, Francisco Duran, sprayed about two dozen bullets from an AK47 rifle into the White House wall before being wrestled to the ground by passers-by. Nobody, not even the would-be assassin, was hurt. Mr Clinton was in the White House this time, watching football on the television, so technically it could be described as an attempt on the life of the President. Another six weeks later, on 17 December, four shots were fired at around two in the morning at the White House, where the President and Mrs Clinton were both in residence. They slept through it all, and nobody was ever arrested in what may well have been a 'drive-by' shooting. Just three days later, a 33-year-old homeless man named Marcelino Corniel was shot and killed by police after he wielded a knife on Pennsylvania Avenue next to the North Lawn of the White House, but once again Mr Clinton, who was in the Oval Office at the time, was unaware of all that was going on around him.

The only President to resign was, of course, Richard Nixon in 1974, in the wake of the Watergate affair. Andrew Johnson, Abraham Lincoln's Vice-President who took over after the assassination, is the only President to have faced an impeachment trial, largely because it was deemed that he had dismissed his Secretary of War, Edwin Stanton, on 21 February 1868 in violation of a Congressional law. The president *pro tempore* of the Senate, Ben Wade, who was next in line to the Presidency, was so confident that Johnson would be found guilty that he had already selected a Cabinet, but in the end Johnson was exonerated by the vote of Senator Edmund G. Ross of Kansas, whose 'not guilty' ensured that a large enough majority to convict could not be found.

One of the many foreign journalists covering the impeachment trial was the Frenchman Georges Clemenceau, who was later to become Prime Minister of France, and who had his own individual way of attempting to secure the end of the career of his enemies, whether political or personal. He was a duellist. He fought over 20 duels, both with swords and with

pistols, and had the record of only ever injuring one of his opponents. However, he too was never seriously injured in a duel, and thus it can be assumed that these affairs were truly a matter of honour, not a matter of physical supremacy. One of his opponents was Paul Deschanel, who was elected President of the French Republic in 1920, none the worse for having come up against Clemenceau in the early dawn light. Clemenceau also acted as second to Charles Floquet, the 60-year-old President of the French Council of Ministers, when he was challenged to a duel in 1888 by the unstable Georges Boulanger, one-time Minister of War. Boulanger, over ten years younger than Floquet and a military man, should have been able to win the duel easily, but instead he was wounded and the shame of the defeat put paid to schemes he was harbouring to install himself as a military dictator of France. Three years later, he committed suicide in Brussels as his creditors closed in on him.

Political figures do eventually retire and die, not necessarily in that order, although it is a curious fact that, as that noted political analyst Screaming Lord Sutch points out in his autobiography, 'The number of by-elections has been steadily decreasing over this century, partly because MPs are fitter and younger.' Not all MPs are as fit and young for their age as Teresa Gorman, who was short-listed as Conservative candidate for Billericay in 1987. Although she was then 55, almost 56 years old, she was a champion of hormone replacement therapy and chairman of Amarant, a charity for 'better health care for mature women', and she was determined to be selected to contest the seat. Accordingly, she gave the impression that she was several years younger, and was selected. Even after winning the seat for the Conservatives, she was reluctant to reveal her exact age. In the 1990 edition of *Dod's Parliamentary Companion*, the guide to who is who in Westminster, she was still giving her year of birth as 1937, but shortly thereafter official publications reverted to giving her date of birth as 30 September 1931, showing how rapidly life as an MP can age a person.

Fitness is vital for any politician. The astronaut and American hero John Glenn had to withdraw from the 1964 Senate race when he fell in his bathtub and injured himself. It was another ten years before he finally became one of the Senators from Ohio. Most politicians try to keep their state of health a secret from the general public. President Wilson was a virtual vegetable after his stroke in October 1919, while his wife and his doctor shielded him from the outside world and the outside world from the truth of his condition; and President Pompidou's final illness was hidden from the public until very near the end. Few are unlucky enough to have books written about them after their death by their doctor, as both Chairman Mao and Sir Winston Churchill did. However, as Dr Zhisui Li and Lord Moran kept their patients alive and active until well beyond the officially approved three score years and ten, they were well served in life if not in death. Churchill's fitness regime apparently consisted of cigars and alcohol, while Mao lived in total ignorance of the invention of the toothbrush. He also had his way until late in old age with any young woman who caught his eye, and many did. Other politicians have followed his example.

Most parliaments now have gymnasia attached, where even the most sluggish member can make a pretence of working out. The British Parliament's gym has an annual membership subscription of £200, and fewer than ten per cent of all MPs are members. The life of an MP is extraordinarily stressful and filled with large meals, constituency cocktail parties, routine late-night sessions, not to mention hectic travelling to and from the constituency every weekend. Jo Grimond, when MP for the Orkneys and Shetlands, reckoned to travel 75,000 miles a year between London and his constituency, although he was noted for his strong constitution and lived into his eighties. Other MPs take in their stride the 'broken marriages, ruined health and exhausted irrationality' which Edwina Currie MP described as the natural consequence of being an MP. It is all part of the price to pay for a share in the wielding of power.

If they are too ashamed of their bodies to share their flab with colleagues (or if, like Betty Boothroyd, they feel that working out in the gym is somehow beneath the dignity of Madam Speaker), they can always just plug in a video in the privacy of their own home and follow the instructions. There are even dangers here, though. One would-be slimmer in the 1980s was reported to have refused to participate in a Weight Watchers' class because the particular fitness video they were using, which would have helped her to lose several pounds of cellulite and tone up those sagging muscles, featured a fitness instructor who reminded her of Mrs Thatcher.

Tobacco and loose women are two of the major health risks to which politicians succumb, with at least one notable politician of the past few years having died while in the intimate embrace of his 'research assistant', but drink is the true demon. Sean O'Casey once wrote: 'A man should be drunk when he talks politics. It's the only way to make them important'. Several people have taken him at his word. An unnamed member of the New Zealand Parliament in the early years of the century entered the House one evening during an important announcement by his Prime Minister, sat down, took off his boots, placed them on the Treasury table and immediately went to sleep, 'snoring like a foghorn', according to a contemporary report. He was the member for a dry constituency.

An MP at Westminster is not allowed to describe another member as 'drunk', but a number of euphemisms have emerged over the years to point out that the member in question is not in full control of his or her words and actions. Alan Clark,

in his diaries, describes one of his first sessions answering questions from the front benches, as a junior minister at the Department of Employment, in July 1983. The session came immediately after a 'wine-tasting' dinner, and Clare Short MP soon pointed out that the minister, if not drunk, was certainly incapable. Clark is far less guilty than many other members over the years, notably George Brown, the Labour MP for Belper who was Foreign Secretary in Harold Wilson's Cabinet, and who had a tendency to fall over at official functions. Wilson came from a political family, but even before young Harold was born, they knew of the dangers of mixing drink and politicians. Wilson's uncle was chairman of the North West Manchester Liberal Party in 1908 when their sitting MP, Winston Churchill, was appointed to the Cabinet. At that time, all newly appointed cabinet ministers had to resign and seek re-election, which Churchill duly did. Unfortunately, the good citizens of North West Manchester decided to take the opportunity to unseat Mr Churchill, and elected William Joynson-Hicks, the Conservative candidate, by 429 votes. After the result was announced, the defeated candidate sat in the constituency headquarters with tears streaming down his face. The only consolation he could find was in a succession of large whiskies, which Harold Wilson's uncle, a strict teetotaller, found himself having to pay for. Churchill moved up to Dundee, where he fought and won a by-election for the Liberals, no doubt fortified in the knowledge that he was representing a part of the homeland of his favourite consolatory drink.

Andrew Johnson, Lincoln's Vice-President, was so drunk when he took the oath of office in March 1865 that he could barely repeat the words that the Chief Justice was reading out to him. His excuse was that he was drinking to ease the pain of a bout of typhoid fever, but this did not impress the local pressmen. The *New York World* was blunt: 'One frail life stands between this insolent clownish creature and the presidency. May God bless and spare Abraham Lincoln.' Barely six weeks later, Lincoln was dead and Johnson was President. The *New York World* was right: Johnson did not honour the office he held. Other American politicians have fought a hard battle with alcohol over the years, including Jim Folsom, the Governor of Alabama, who appeared to be so drunk on television just before the Democratic primary election in 1962 that he even forgot the names of his own children. He also gave what was described as 'an extended imitation of a cuckoo clock'. He lost the election. Wilbur Mills, then Chairman of the House Ways and Means Committee, and one of the most powerful men on Capitol Hill, was stopped for speeding in Washington in 1974. His companion in the car, a stripper named Fanne Foxe, ended up in the Tidal Basin while Mills tried to explain to the police what exact government research project he was involved in which required him to drive at excess speeds with excess of alcohol in his blood and excess of stripper in his car. Two months later Mills appeared on stage with Miss Foxe at a strip show in Boston. Fortunately, he kept his clothes about him, if not his dignity or his political career.

Spectacular drunkenness in our politicians is still with us. Boris Yeltsin was officially reported to have been suffering from high blood pressure when he failed to appear from his aircraft after a flight from Seattle to Shannon on 30 September 1994. The Irish Prime Minister Albert Reynolds waited patiently

on the tarmac, but the scheduled stopover had apparently become a sleepover, and Mr Yeltsin never made it on to the Irish sod. This was not the first example of Mr Yeltsin's irregular behaviour. His first American visit, in 1989, became known as the 'bourbon trip', and a month or two later he presented himself at a Moscow police station, soaked to the skin, claiming to have been pushed into the river. On an official trip to Germany, he seized the baton from a brass band conductor and led the musicians in an unrecognizable tune, which was not, however, a Russian drinking song. He has delivered several incoherent speeches, including one to the Duma in 1993, which makes his performance in power a strong contrast to that of his predecessor, Mikhail Gorbachev, whose first months in power were marked by edicts limiting the amount of vodka to be consumed by bureaucrats, with an accompanying increase in both governmental efficiency and ministerial long faces.

Drugs have been less of a personal problem for politicians, although they have managed to blame every evil of modern society on the influence of drugs on our young people. In certain countries, such as Colombia, Pakistan and Thailand, the production of drugs has become a major foreign currency earner, while America remains the major market for all mind-expanding chemical substances. In the 1970s President Nixon assumed that the anti-war sentiments of the student generation were linked to the fact that they were obviously all on drugs, and so when the opportunity arose, he sought the help of a man who was not only free from any taint of drug-taking, but was also a hero to the youth of 1970 (or at least those who regularly attended Las Vegas night-club shows), Elvis Presley. It was not enough that Vice-President Spiro Agnew was fulminating in speeches against the pernicious message of the song 'Puff the Magic Dragon', Richard Nixon needed to get youth on his side. Nixon met the 35-year-old Presley at the White House on 21 December 1970, in a meeting engineered by Elvis, who collected badges and wanted one from the Department of Justice Bureau of Narcotics and Dangerous Drugs. Elvis got what he wanted, but his occasional statements from the stages of Las Vegas that drugs were bad did not give Nixon any assurance that he had got much out of the deal. But even after Elvis had died from the effects of prolonged drug abuse, the President defended him as having only ever used prescription drugs, and never cocaine or other less legal items.

Marion Barry, the Democrat Mayor of Washington, succeeded in a remarkable come-back from the political grave when in 1994 he was re-elected to his job five years after leaving in disgrace, having been videotaped taking crack in a hotel room. Come-backs are rare in politics, but they have been achieved. Richard Nixon lost the race to be Governor of

California in 1962, two years after having lost the presidential race to John Kennedy, and he told the Press that they would not have Richard Nixon 'to kick around any more'. Six years later, he was elected President. Winston Churchill and Harold Macmillan are examples of British politicians who went on to lead their party and their country despite having at one stage lost the party whip, and Alexander Dubcek came back from complete obscurity after his overthrow in the wake of the 1968 Russian invasion of Prague to become Speaker of the Czech Parliament at the time of his death. In December 1994 it was reported that William Hill had taken about £750 in bets from one unnamed man who was backing former Chancellor Norman Lamont to become next leader of the Conservative Party. At odds of 33–1, this was one come-back that even the cautious people behind a bookmakers' grille thought was very unlikely indeed.

If a British MP wishes to resign, the only way he can do it is by applying for the stewardship of the Manor of Northstead, or for the Chiltern Hundreds, which are theoretically offices of profit under the Crown: holders of such offices are barred from being Members of Parliament. However, there is something about life at Westminster which makes MPs reluctant to resign even when urged to do so, or even when they have promised to do so. Eric Leslie Gandar Dower, who could well have appeared among these Curiosities much earlier, as an actor turned politician, perhaps, or as one of a pair of brothers in Parliament together (Col. Alan Gandar Dower was Tory MP for Cumberland and Penrith at the same time that Eric was Tory MP for Caithness and Sutherland), or even as an aviator and businessman, the only MP to own his own airline –

actually gets his mention for refusing to resign his seat. He was elected in the July 1945 election, apparently on the promise that he would resign as soon as the Japanese surrendered. This they did in August 1945, but Mr Gandar Dower stayed on. In December 1946 he promised to resign on the marriage of his secretary. But Mr Gandar Dower stayed on. In February 1947 Lady Violet Bonham Carter pointed out in a letter to *The Times:* 'Japan has been defeated, and Mr Gandar Dower's secretary, we are glad to know, has been duly married, but Mr Gandar Dower has not carried out his pledge to the electors of Caithness and Sutherland.' Gandar Dower's excuse was that 'my resignation was submitted for business reasons which are not now so cogent', and he stayed at Westminster until the next general election, in 1950.

Death is God's way of telling a politician the debate is over and voting has started. The best way to end life's great debate was found by Senator Alben Barkley, the Kentucky Democrat who had been Senate majority leader for 10 years and President Truman's Vice-President from 1949 to 1953. On 30 April

1956 he was taking part in a mock Democratic Party convention at Washington and Lee University in Lexington, Virginia. He was speaking from the podium to a packed auditorium, and had just told his audience that he would 'rather be a servant in the house of the Lord than sit in the seat of the mighty'. No sooner had he spoken than his wish was granted. He staggered and fell to the floor, having suffered a massive heart attack. Doctors administered oxygen, but it was too late. Senator Barkley's body was carried out on a stretcher while the students sat in stunned silence. Then Paul Holstein, Mayor of Lexington, who had been sharing the platform with Mr Barkley, stepped forward and told the gathering that he believed it would have been the Senator's wish not to have the convention cut short. So they carried on. In politics, as in life, the show must go on.

SUPPLEMENTARIES

Politicians who died at sea:

Harold Holt, Prime Minister of Australia, disappeared while scuba diving, 17 December 1967.

Hector Hughes QC, former Labour MP for Aberdeen North, died on 23 June 1970 after being rescued from the Channel at Brighton, aged 82.

James Ramsay MacDonald, former Prime Minister of the UK, died of a heart attack on board the *Reina del Pacifico* on 9 November 1937, while heading for a holiday in the mountains of Peru.

Robert Maxwell, former Labour MP for Buckingham, died after falling off his yacht, the *Lady Ghislaine*, in the Atlantic on 5 November 1991.

Politicians who wanted us to think they died at sea:

John Stonehouse, Labour MP, faked his own suicide by drowning, USA 1974.

Politicians who died at Number 10 Downing Street:

Sir Henry Campbell-Bannerman died on 22 April 1908, having resigned as Prime Minister on 5 April 1908.

Politicians who died on 9 November include:

Ramsay MacDonald, 1937

Neville Chamberlain, 1940

Chaim Weizmann, 1952

Charles de Gaulle, 1970

Politicians who died on 24 January include:

Randolph Churchill, 1895

Sir Winston Churchill, 1965

Politicians who died on 6 June 1968:

Randolph Churchill, former Conservative MP for Preston

Senator Robert Kennedy, former US Attorney-General

Politicians killed in air crashes:

Rep. Larry P. McDonald died when KAL jumbo jet shot down, 1 September 1983

Lord Thomson, Secretary of State for Air, R101 airship disaster, 5 October 1930

Cyprien Ntaryamira, President of Burundi, and Juvenal Habyarimana, President of Rwanda, died when their plane was shot down, 6 April 1994

President Zia ul-Haq of Pakistan, August 1988

Vladislav Sikorski, Prime Minister in exile of Poland, in Gibraltar, 1943

Sanjay Gandhi, Indian Congress Party MP, 1980

Politicians attacked but not killed by would-be assassins:

Gerald Ford, President of USA, was attacked by Lynette 'Squeaky' Fromme on 5 September 1975 and by Jane Moore on 22 September 1975. He was unharmed.

Vladimir Ilyich Lenin was shot in the neck and shoulder on 30 August 1918.

Bernardette McAliskey, former MP, was shot and wounded by Protestant gunmen, Co. Tyrone, 16 January 1981.

Augusto Pinochet, President of Chile, escaped unharmed when his motorcade was attacked by rockets, bazookas, grenades and rifles, 7 September 1986.

President Ronald Reagan was shot and wounded by John W. Hinckley in Washington, 30 March 1981.

Margaret Thatcher, Prime Minister of the UK, was unharmed when an IRA bomb exploded at the Grand Hotel in Brighton, 12 October 1984.

Governor George Wallace was shot by Arthur Bremer and paralysed at an election rally, 15 May 1972.

French Presidents who have died in office:

François Faure, 1899

Georges Pompidou, 1974

Politicians who committed suicide:

Pierre Beregovoy, former Prime Minister of France, 1 May 1993

George Ernest Jean-Marie Boulanger, former French Minister of War, 30 September 1891

Adolf Hitler, Führer of Germany, 30 April 1945

President Getulio Vargas of Brazil, 24 August 1954

Long-lived Prime Ministers:

Prince Naruhiko Higashikuni, Prime Minister of Japan for two months in 1945, died on 20 January 1990, aged 102 years 1 month.

Christopher Hornsrud, Prime Minister of Norway for eighteen days in 1928, died on 13 December 1960, aged 101 years 1 month.

Antoine Pinay, Prime Minister of France for seven months in 1952, died on 13 December 1994, 17 days before his 103rd birthday.

Politicians in power after the age of 90:

Dr Hastings Banda, President of Malawi from 1964 to 1994, aged about 96

Deng Xiaoping, China's head of state in 1995, aged 91

Jozsef Madarasz, Member of Hungarian Parliament for 47 years between 1832 and his death in 1915, aged 101

Senator Strom Thurmond, Chairman of the US Senate Armed Services Committee, in 1995, aged 92